GR 221

Mallorca's Long Distance Trail

'Ruta de Pedra en Sec'
'Dry Stone Way'

with

Charles Davis

DISCOVERY WALKING GUIDES LTD

GR221 Mallorca's Long Distance Trail
'The Dry Stone Way'

First Edition - May 2009
Copyright © 2009

Published by
Discovery Walking Guides Ltd
10 Tennyson Close, Northampton NN5 7HJ,
England

Photographs
All photographs in this book were taken by the
author Charles Davis.

Maps
Created from Mallorca North & Mountains
Tour & Trail Map plus additional mapping by
David Brawn © David Brawn 2009

Cover Photos;
A Dragonera Stage1, B Coll del Ofre Stage 6,
C Archdukes Path Stage 4, D Cliffs north of
Puig Veia Stage 3

ISBN 9781904946489
Text and photographs © Charles Davis 2009
Maps & Altitude Profiles © David Brawn
2009

GR 221 Mallorca's Long Distance Walking Route

CONTENTS

Charles Davis was born in London, and has lived and worked in the United States, Sudan, Turkey, Ivory Coast, Spain and France. With the onset of middle age, he realised that the urge to roam was better satisfied by walking than bouncing about on the back of a lorry in the middle of the desert, and now divides his time between mountain tops, desk-tops and laptops.

Following his successful, and highly acclaimed, series of Walk! guide books Charles has drawn on his extensive knowledge of Mallorca to research and write the first book dedicated to the GR221 *Ruta de Pedra en Sec* 'Dry Stone Way' long distance hiking route. Accompanied by Jeanette Tallegas on his adventure Charles has produced another classic that combines his illuminating insights into Mallorcan life with the detailed walk descriptions that will enable you to recreate this most memorable of Mallorcan challenges.

Jeanette Tallegas has spent thirty odd years labouring for the French education system, from which she has finally, gleefully, taken early retirement. Asked what she intends doing now, she resolutely replies, "Nothing". Nonetheless, she does follow the author up various gruelling mountains, frequently alarming younger walkers who seem to assume that remote and inaccessible places are the preserve of youth.

Charles Davis is also the author of:-

Walk! Mallorca North & Mountains	ISBN 9781904946496
Walk! the Alpujarras	ISBN 9781904946236
Walk! Mallorca West	ISBN 9781899554980
Walk! La Gomera	ISBN 9781899554904
Walk! La Palma	ISBN 9781904946069
Walk! Andorraa	ISBN 9781904946045
Walk! the Axarquía	ISBN 9781904946083
Walk! the Lake District South	ISBN 9781904946168
Walk! Dorset	ISBN 9781904946205
Walk! Brittany (North)	ISBN 9781904946359
Bumping About Brittany	ISBN 9781904946441

- published by **Discovery Walking Guides Ltd.**

Walk On, Bright Boy	ISBN 9781579621537	Permanent Press
Walking The Dog	ISBN 9781579621674	Permanent Press
Costa del Sol Walks	ISBN 8489954399	Santana
Costa Blanca Walks	ISBN 9788489954571	Santana

When it comes to walking, size matters. I offer this observation not in a spirit of witless macho braggadocio, nor as an evocation of those romantic nineteenth century ramblers who would pop out for a post-prandial stroll and only really felt they were beginning to limber up by the time they'd got their first thirty miles under the belt. But no matter how exquisite a short itinerary may be, it can never compare to a really big walk on a long distance path.

This is the sort of walking that becomes a way of being, not only abstracting one from the petty cares of getting by, getting ahead and getting on in the world, but turning into the very reason for life itself, so that one's only concerns are what lies over the brow of the next hill, the only thought as one falls asleep being for the next day's walking, the next day's progress, until eventually, when one stops to 'take a day off', a couple of hours idleness are enough to have you asking yourself, "What am I doing lounging about here? Why aren't I walking?"

'GALATZÓ, emblematic mountain of the southwest (Stage Two)

The combination, therefore, of a long distance path and Europe's favourite warm island walking destination is enough to excite any dedicated walker, and it's no mere marketing ploy to say that the present publication has come about by popular demand. Time and again, readers of our guidebooks to Mallorca (Walk! Mallorca North & Mountains and Walk! Mallorca West) have asked about the GR221, why it hasn't featured more prominently in previous publications, why it hasn't been detailed on the Tour & Trail map, where they can get more information, and so forth.

The simple answer to all these questions is that, though the projected route was known and some of it signposted, there were long stretches without any wayposting whatsoever, several places where the authorities were still negotiating rights-of-way, a couple of instances where access to private land was, potentially at least, sufficiently confrontational to spoil the whole trip, and only two refuges existed along the entire route, a route that a group of local 'walkers' knock off in a single weekend once a year, but which would take most of us at least a week.

Some of these problems persist, albeit to an ever diminishing degree, and there are parts of the present itinerary that will probably change in the coming years, but the path has now developed enough to justify publishing a book about what should, by any criteria, count as one of Europe's great walking experiences.

Cobbled trails are characteristic of the 'Dry Stone Way' (Stage Three)

GR221 - The Dry Stone Way

Anybody who has visited **Mallorca**, either for a dedicated walking holiday or as a casual tourist, will appreciate the justice of the GR221's official title and the name by which it is better known on the island, *La Ruta de Pedra en Sec*, for **Mallorca** is defined by dry stone. The island itself is the rocky extremity of the Baetic Cordillera, surging out of the sea like the gnarled tip of some petrified sea monster's tail, and the preponderance of stone has determined a large part of its history, from the Talayotic culture of the Bronze Age with its distinctive stone shelters and weapon of choice (the slingshot, with which the islanders were so lethally adept that one etymological interpretation cites the slingshot as the source of the word balear) to the modern day and the magnificent stone farmhouses that have lured countless well-heeled northern Europeans to the island in search of their own particular place in the sun.

Dragonerra (Stage One)

Following ancient bridleways along the length of the **Tramuntana** range, from **Port d'Andratx** in the southwest to **Pollença** in the northeast, the GR221 touches upon dry stone in its every manifestation, from the raw rock of the peaks and sweeping fields of karst to the tailored stones that have always been Mallorca's natural building material. In some cases, we use immaculately paved trails, notably on the famous pilgrims' paths around Mallorca's spiritual heartland at **Lluc** (Stages Seven & Eight) and on the classic donkey trail up the **Barranc de Biniaraix** (Stage Six), at other times we walk along bare rock below looming cliffs, and everywhere we cross the rocky passes that have always been the portals between the island's otherwise isolated communities.

En route, we pass the remains of the stone huts and the stone-clad firing circles used by charcoal burners; we see dry-stone springs, dry-stone cisterns, dry-stone snow-pits, dry-stone retaining walls, dry-stone drinking troughs, dry-stone limekilns, dry-stone byres, dry-stone stiles, dry-stone bread ovens, dry-stone wells, dry-stone sheepfolds, dry-stone aquifers, dry-stone threshing circles . . . basically, anything you can prefix with 'dry-stone', we get it. Perhaps most remarkable of all are the boundary walls dividing the great estates,

Dry Stone Spring, Font des Quer (Stage Two)

often as not raised in places so inaccessible and on such steep gradients that it's hard to believe people were willing let alone able to get there, and the notion that they were both willing and able and then still had the insouciance to hang about piling stones into a straight line that would hold fast for centuries, well, that's strictly for the birds . . . and us.

Bird's eye view, Estellencs (Stage Three)

That, of course, is the distinctive appeal of the *Ruta de Pedra en Sec*, the fact that it takes walkers into places most tourists never see and offers us a bird's eye view of this magnificent landscape, giving visitors a complete picture of the **Tramuntana** range in a single holiday, freeing one from the commonplace constraints of time and transport, and lending a coherence to the experience that day walks can only achieve over the course of a far longer and far more costly trip.

And if, after the dry-stone catalogue above, you're beginning to think you're going to have dry stones up to your eyeballs, which would inevitably be a bit of a pain in the neck, never fear because there is enough adventure and variety crammed into this trail to keep one entertained on an itinerary twice as long, the many manifestations of dry stone being broken up by plains of citrus groves, terraces of ancient olive trees, fabulous forests of Holm Oak, exquisite pastoral enclaves tucked away in secluded corners, and spectacular valleys and ravines laced with the glittering threads of mountain torrents, all of it backed by the broad blue palette of the Mediterranean.

Starting from **Port d'Andratx** in the southwest of the island, the GR221 crosses the **Pas Vermell**, then descends to the former fishing port at **Sant Elm** before climbing to the ruined monastery at **La Trapa** overlooking the extraordinary little island of **Sa Dragonera**. It then climbs to the **Coll de sa Gramola** and skirts the two great peaks of the west, **S'Esclop** (929m) and **Galatzó** (1027m), en route to **Estellencs**.

S'Esclop (Stage Two)

After **Banyalbufar**, it follows the celebrated *Camí des Correu* to **Esporles**, then passes through **Valldemossa** and takes the even more famous *Camí de s'Arxiduc* to **Deià**, from where an easy walk brings us into the **Sóller** valley at the foot of the island's major mountains. These are accessed by dint of a steady slog up the classic **Barranc de Biniaraix** trail to the **Ofre** estate and the central reservoirs of **Cúber** and **Gorg Blau,** where we do the tour of **Tossals Verds.**

From here, the itinerary passes between Mallorca's highest peaks, **Puig Major** (1447m) and **Puig de Massanella** (1382m) then drops down to **Lluc** and the monastery that is the object of the island's main pilgrimages, after which a gentle descent on the popular *Carretera Vella* brings us to **Pollença** and the end of the trail.

Gorg Blau (Stage Six)

The eight official stages of the itinerary are:

1.	**Port d'Andratx to La Trapa**	10km
2.	**La Trapa to Coma d'en Vidal (nr. Estellencs)**	14km
3.	**Coma d'en Vidal to Esporles**	18km
4.	**Esporles to Can Boi (Deià)**	16km
5.	**Can Boi to La Muleta (Sóller)**	8.5km
6.	**La Muleta to Tossals Verds**	21km
7.	**Tossals Verds to Son Amer (Lluc)**	14km
8.	**Son Amer to Pollença**	14.5km

In addition to this main itinerary, there are a number (between three and ten according to who you're talking to!) of options/alternative routes. The two principal official variants on the main trail are between Stages Four & Six (Valldemossa to Tossals Verds) and Stages Five & Seven (Muleta to Son Amer).

Variant 1: Valldemossa to **Tossals Verds** heads southeast to **Bunyola** then shadows the road to **Orient** before climbing to **Castell de Alaró** and embarking on another long bout of road walking to reach **Tossals Verds** via the **Almedra** access lane. Although mostly passable, this option is still in the project stage and has not been detailed in the present volume because of access restrictions, the amount of road walking, and the fact that the main route to the north is undisputed, well-established, clearly waymarked, and more attractive! However, once finalized, the **Valldemossa-Tossals Verds** alternative should make a useful option for a four day circular route.

Variant 2: Muleta to **Son Amer**. Climbing to the famous **Mirador de ses Barques** then following the popular **Sa Costera** trail to **Cala Tuent** and **Sa Calobra** this is an interesting option, as it would allow walkers with

Es Cornadors (Stage Six)

some scrambling experience to venture into the **Torrent de Pareis**, Europe's second largest gorge. At the time of writing, the path (indicated on the *Consell de Mallorca* website) climbing alongside and crisscrossing the spectacular **Nus de Corbata** road toward **Lluc** doesn't exist.

NOTE: Given the pace of progress thus far in developing the main route of the GR221, I very much doubt either of these variants will exist in any other than notional form for a considerable time to come.

State of the Route & Options

At the time of going to press, the official route is uncontested and clearly sign and wayposted from **Deià** (Stage Five) to **Pollença** (Stage Eight). The early stages are still in various phases of development.

> **Stage One**. This crosses private land via undisputed, well-established trails. There are no GR specific signposts, but pathfinding is not a problem.

> **Stage Two** involves crossing private property where the rights-of-way are still being negotiated and there are significant pathfinding problems.

> **Stage Three**. The first part between **Estellencs** and **Banyalbufar** has been cut at the **Es Rafal** estate, forcing walkers back onto the road. The local authorities are challenging the legal ruling that has allowed this and the *Consell de Mallorca* is in the process of buying the neighbouring **Planícia** estate where a new route may be feasible. The second part of Stage Three (**Banyalbufar** to **Esporles**) is uncontested and clearly way and signposted throughout with GR-specific wayposts.

> **Stage Four**. GR signposting for the first part (**Esporles** to **Valldemossa**) is incomplete, however there are only two points at which pathfinding is slightly problematic. The second part (**Valldemossa** to **Deià**) has no GR-specific signposting, but the route follows clear, well-established trails.

It had been my intention to work out alternative routes avoiding the problem areas, but after a couple of fruitless days fluffing about in the mountains I realized that the natural alternatives were either ludicrously arduous or even more controversial than the conventional itinerary. Once **Planícia** is bought by the government, it should be relatively easy to by-pass **Es Rafal**, but while **Planícia** remains in private hands it didn't seem reasonable to publish one trespass as an option to another. Hopefully though, the public interest will prevail and the ancient right-of-way through **Es Rafal** will be reopened. In the event that it is reopened, the old route is described in the present publication.

I have also included five unofficial variants:

two alternative starts (from **Es Capdella** and **Puigpunyent**);

two off-trail accommodation options in Stages One & Two;

and a more direct and more interesting route between the **Cúber** reservoir and the **Tossals Verds** refuge (Stage Six).

Pas Llis, the alternative route to Tossals Verds (Stage Six)

NOTE: Unlike most GRs, the symbolic colours of the GR221 are mostly (though not always, the end of Stage Seven bucks the trend) red-and-yellow rather than the standard red-and-white, presumably in honour of the Spanish and Catalan flags. The colours appear on sign and wayposts, but as with most walks on the island, the preferred method of waymarking between principal junctions is cairns (yup, dry stone!), not painted waymarks.

Cala de Deià (Stage Five)

Apart from the state of the paths, another vital consideration when you're planning your trip is where you're going to lay your head for the night. In theory, each stage of the route ends at a government run refuge with a full range of services. In practice, not all the refuges are open or even built (though hopefully this will change before the current edition of this book is updated) and not everyone will want to opt for dormitory accommodation.

That said, if the words 'refuge' and 'dormitory' put you in mind of some shabby, semi-ruinous shack steeped in dust and unidentifiable detritus and filled with a pall of greasy smoke as rowdy bands of drunken adolescents delicately scorch sausages and lightly char raw chicken over open fires (all right, I'm exaggerating slightly, but you know the sort of thing I'm talking about), or a massive room stuffed to the gills with a lot of grimy strangers snuffling and snorting and making other hopefully anonymous noises in the dark of the night, think again.

The *Consell de Mallorca* refuges are beautifully appointed places, immaculately kept, serving food of a standard that draws in the day-trippers as much as the long-distance-hikers, and providing comfortable accommodation in small clean dormitories. In fact, if you're walking with friends, you can probably expect to have a room to yourselves. Moreover, not all the beds are bunk beds and in **Tossals Verds** you can even book a private room for two. And if the regulations specifying no booze can be brought onto the premises suggest you're in for an experience as dry as the name of the GR, don't panic. The bars are well stocked.

The Son Amer Refuge (Stage Seven)

Refuges must be booked at least five days in advance, but given their popularity, it is best if you book as far ahead as possible. Bookings are accepted up to two months in advance. Until very recently, the only way one could book was by calling (in Catalan or Spanish!) (00-34) 971 173 700 or 971 173 731. Happily, this has now changed and there is a simple, on-line booking service ...

www.conselldemallorca.cat/mediambient/pedra/senderisme.php?opcio=20&reserva=1

Camping or bivouacking is feasible, especially on the last three stages where there are several water supplies, an *área recreativa* where camping is tolerated, a designated camping area, and a number of government owned estates. It is, however, risky on private land. Landowners don't like it, above all if it involves a naked flame, and even in places where it is generally overlooked if you're discreet about it, there's no guarantee that you won't be woken in the middle of the night by somebody waving a torch in your face. Above all, it has to be stressed that in the early stages you can't rely upon camping near a water source, so you have to carry any water you're likely to need. The only really reliable spring on Stages One to Four is in the car-park at the western end of **Estellencs**.

Sant Elm (Stage 1)

Here, in brief, is a resumé of accommodation options.

Stage One - to **La Trapa**. Work is still ongoing on the **La Trapa** Refuge and there are no immediate alternatives. This implies either a very short first day, staying over in **Sant Elm** before a very long second day, or a longish first day descending to **S'Arraco** (our preferred option) then taxiing up on day two to rejoin the official route. It is also possible to stay at **Andratx**.

Stage Two - to **Estellencs**. Restoration of the **Coma d'en Vidal** farmhouse near **Estellencs** was completed in 2007, but the refuge has yet to be opened. However, there are several hotels in **Estellencs**.

Stage Three - to **Esporles**. There is no refuge in **Esporles** at present, but again, there is one very attractive hotel and several *agroturismos* (upmarket B&Bs). There are also numerous hotels in **Banyalbufar**.

Stage Four - to **Deià**. The **Can Boi** refuge is up and running in **Deià**, and there is alternative accommodation in **Valldemossa** and **Deià**.

Stage Five - to **Sóller**. **La Muleta** refuge has been operating for several years and there are plenty of hotels in **Sóller** and **Port de Sóller**.

Stage Six - to **Tossals Verds**. Apart from camping or getting the key for the unmanned **Cúber** refuge (in practice not a realistic option), there is no alternative accommodation to the **Tossals Verds** refuge.

Stage Seven - to **Lluc**. The **Son Amer** refuge is operational, alternative accommodation is available at the **Lluc** monastery. There is also a camping area.

Stage Eight - to **Pollença**. The **Pont Romá** refuge at **Pollença** is operational and there is plenty of alternative accommodation in the town.

Ancient olive trees are seen throughout the GR221

For a guide to accommodation en route, see Appendix B, for updates see:-
.

the updates section on Discovery Walking Guides' website at www.walking.demon.co.uk

the news and GR221 pages on the very useful walking website run by a couple of Mallorcan mountain guides - http://idd02ucg.eresmas.net/hike.htm

and the section of the local government site dealing with the GR221 www.conselldemallorca.net/mediambient/pedra.

Since we were camping, the accommodation 'recommendations' are restricted to a simple guide and sometimes a recommendation from our readers or local sources. We would greatly appreciate it if you could give us some feedback on your experiences, good or bad, of services en route. Hopefully, as time goes on, we can build up a data-base of readers' experiences that will serve as an online guide to services. I suspect that most of the places listed will prove adequate if not good. My own experience suggests that when you're on a long distance path, anywhere that offers hot water, a bed, and above all the opportunity to fill your stomach is perceived as a veritable palace.

Wild goats are seen frequently

Structure of the Book

Given that the early stages of the itinerary are still being developed and that there will inevitably be small changes in the precise route followed as new paths are cleared and new refuges are opened, we have stuck with the basic eight stage format for ease of reference when checking for developments in the official source material. However, though the numbering remains the same, we have made the following variations:

Stage One includes a section of the climb to **Coll de sa Gramola** (officially part of Stage Two) and a descent to **S'Arraco** for accommodation, the best non-camping option until the **La Trapa** refuge opens.

Stage Two includes a description of the descent to **Estellencs** (officially part of Stage Three) since the **Coma d'en Vidal** refuge has yet to be opened.

Stage Five includes a description of the descent from the **Muleta** plateau to **Sóller** town (officially part of Stage Six) since Five is a short stage and I suspect most people will want to do a little extra walking prior to the rigors of Stage Six.

For various reasons (sometimes practical, sometimes simply because it seemed more desirable) detailed in the respective introductions, Stages One, Three, Four & Six have each been broken into two sections.

Interleaved with the main text you will find 'Gobbets' and 'Town Sketches'. These have no relevance to pathfinding or doing the walk, but give background information that may help those unfamiliar with **Mallorca** extract a little more pleasure from the experience. For planning purposes, appendices summarize distances and services en route, the various accommodation options, the availability of public transport, links to itineraries in other Discovery Walking Guides, and sources of ancillary information.

The book was researched piecemeal rather than as a straightforward LDP, which may suggest my timings would be unreasonably fast since I was walking with a day pack rather than a full rucksack. However, I think the burden was comparable since I was generally carrying a computer plus food, drink and water for two people and two dogs. Bear in mind, though, these are all 'pure' times, discounting stopping, snacking, snapping, and simply standing still staring open-mouthed at the unfolding spectacle, an inactivity in which I tend to indulge to a degree resembling imbecility.

Ofre (Stage Six)

In the case of the *Ruta de Pedra en Sec*, 'at the beginning' is not necessarily the obvious answer. A few points to consider:

Stage One is lovely, but in its present form Stage Two is only really recommended for people with experience of walking in **Mallorca**.

The first part of Stage Three, the contested route between **Estellencs** and **Banyalbufar**, is best skipped until the **Es Rafal** path is reopened. Fortunately, there is a regular bus-service between the two towns.

In view of the current difficulties with accommodation, rights of way, and pathfinding (none of which are insuperable of themselves, but combined they're a bit irritating), I'd recommend newcomers to the island begin their walk in **Banyalbufar**.

Those of you already familiar with the west of the island might like to consider one of the alternative starts from **Es Capdella** or **Puigpunyent**.

If you're relying on refuges for accommodation (the hotels are generally pricey) start in **Esporles** or **Valldemossa** (depending on how much walking you're prepared to do on the day of arrival).

In all cases, read the introductions for each stage and check out Appendices A & B before making your final decision about which possible starting point is best for you.

In the high mountains (Stage Seven)

Any LDP, even a relatively short one like the GR221, requires a certain amount of planning, planning that is in many ways an essential part of the experience, both in anticipatory pleasure and as a way of imagining your way into the walk so that you are psychologically ready for it when you arrive.

You will obviously need to read through the outline of each stage and decide whether you wish to follow the main itinerary or one of our options, break stages into two parts, or recombine parts of various stages in different ways. There are, however, a number of other considerations. Though most of what follows may seem self-evident, these are the sort of things that are frequently overlooked, sometimes to the great detriment of a holiday.

First, think about how long you normally walk and decide whether the stages are an appropriate length for your walking habits, bearing in mind that you'll probably be carrying more weight than you would on an ordinary day outing, and possibly be climbing more than you're used to.

Once you've decided on an appropriate length for each day's walk, use the distance and accommodation summaries in the appendices to plan your own stages and then BOOK YOUR ACCOMMODATION in advance. Space in the refuges is limited and I know from experience that there's nothing worse than scrabbling about at the end of a hard day's walking looking for somewhere to sleep - unless, perhaps, it's hurrying through a walk because you're worried about finding a bed for the night.

Think ahead about what you'll be needing in the way of picnics and where you're going to get it. Refuges and hotels can provide picnic lunches, but if you have any particular dietary requirements or preferences, you should plan where to shop en route. Above all, bear in mind that after Stage Five there are no shops, so anything you need for the next three days in the way of luxuries has to be in your backpack when you leave **Sóller**. And if you're relying on GPS navigation, it's advisable to carry all the batteries you're likely to need with you, as not all shops have AAA batteries in stock.

Except for Stages Three, Six, Seven & Eight there is no reliable water supply on the GR, so you should take a large water bottle with you and begin each day with at least a couple of litres of water per person. Fruit juices and soft, 'sport' drinks like Aquarius might seem a little dismal if somebody served them up at the cocktail hour, but on trail they can become the nectar of the Gods, especially on a hot day. Are coffee or tea essential? Better take a thermos then. A corkscrew or Swiss Army knife rarely go amiss, either. All this may seem blazingly obvious, but what is a mere minor oversight on a day-walk can rapidly begin to seem like a vital lack on an LDP.

The balance between travelling light and being adequately equipped is a very subjective one. I tend toward the former, not quite to the degree indulged in by the three-socks-in-circulation brigade (clean sock on left foot, yesterday's clean sock on right foot, third sock hanging from your backpack to dry after being washed the previous evening), but enough to end a short LDP like this with at least one item of clothing quietly fermenting at the bottom of my bag.

In Winter you may need a 'warm coat'.

One basic rule above all others: it is essential to have something clean and dry for the evening (take plenty of stuff sacks or plastic bags for isolating clothes and bedding in your rucksack) even if this means setting off in the morning wearing something clammy that looks like it's developing into an independent life form.

Obviously, what you carry will depend on whether you go earlier or later in the season, but as a general rule, light as possible is best. Ideally, you should be able to squeeze everything into a 35-45 litre rucksack (bearing in mind that capacity varies greatly between different packs that claim the same volume). Here's a basic check list of the clothing I would consider adequate for completing the *Ruta de Pedra en Sec*:

> Four long-sleeved shirts or T-shirts
> Two pairs of trousers, one of which could be shorts in warm weather
> Sweatshirt, fleece or jumper for the evenings, all three if you're walking in the late Autumn or in Winter *
> Windcheater/waterproofs, the latter 100% impermeable in the Autumn or Winter *

Sunhat and sunscreen / warm hat in Winter for the follicularly challenged *
Five pairs of socks
Four sets of underwear
Good boots that you know are comfortable
Pair of lightweight canvas shoes or sandals for the evenings
Towel (can be rented in refuges)
Sleeping bag (bed linen can be rented in refuges)

* If you're going between November and March you need to be equipped with much the same warm and waterproof clothing you would be for a weekend outing in the UK. Chances are you'll carry a lot of excess clothing you never wear, but the opposite doesn't bear thinking about.

For a further discussion of equipment, see our standard advice on Walking Equipment.

Puig Roig (Stage Eight)

The main walking season in **Mallorca** runs from September through to May and the GR ought to be feasible in its entirety for most of that time. However, Winter conditions can be tough and it's not unknown for the high central mountains to be cut off by deep snow. The best months for walking the Dry Stone Way in its entirety are September, early October, April and May. Conditions in November can be perfect, but it's also the month with the highest average precipitation, as we can attest all too well. During January and February the nights are cold, but the daytime temperature is generally pleasant and the skies clear.

Unless you're in a real rush to get started, the simplest thing to do on arriving at the airport is to take bus No. 1 from the arrivals floor across from the car park to Plaza d'Espanya in the capital **Palma**, where buses head out in all directions.

From Plaza d'Espanya, take

> Line 102 for **Port d'Andratx** (Stage One),
> Line 111 for **Es Capdella** (Alternative Stage 1A),
> Line 140 for **Puigpunyent** (Alternative Stage 1B),
> Line 200 for **Esporles** (Stage Four), **Banyalbufar** & **Estellencs** (Stage Three),
> Line 210 for **Valldemossa** and **Deià** (Stage Four),
> Line 210 or 211 for **Sóller** (Stage Five).

See Appendix C for frequency.

'Nuff said. Go forth. Enjoy!

Many of the URLs for information about Mallorca are long and unwieldy. To ease planning, we have posted a page of hyperlinked web addresses on Discovery Walking Guides' website: www.walking.demon.co.uk

Our "Symbols Rating Bar" gives you the key information about a walking route in a quick glance. Remember that "Effort/Exertion" and "Refreshments" are the author's opinion and that "Time" is the walking time without stops.

our rating for effort/exertion:-
1 very easy   **2** easy   **3** average
4 energetic   **5** strenuous

approximate **time** to complete a walk (compare your times against ours early in a walk) - does not include stopping time

approximate walking **distance** in kilometres

approximate **ascents/descents** in metres (N = negligible)

linear route; all GR221 stages are linear routes.

risk of **vertigo**; Stage sections 4B and 6BAlt

refreshments (may be at start or end of a route only)

In addition to the 'What to Take' (pages 20-22) you will need to consider what you need for the day-walking section of your pack. In addition to water it is recommended that you carry some snacks for breaks during your hike and as emergency rations. Good footwear goes without saying along with a hat, sunglasses and loose clothing that gives adequate sun protection.

Often it is the smallest of items that prove the most essential so in addition to a mobile phone, whistle and gps you might consider adding:-
- tweezers and a needle, for extracting splinters.
- lipsalve, which is no luxury when your lips dry out.
- a spare pair of boot laces, these can be put to many emergency uses as well as replacing laces if they break.
Most of all take 'care' so that you reduce the chances of an accident happening to you.

The map sections used in this book have been taken from **Mallorca (North & Mountains) Tour & Trail Map 5th edition** (ISBN 9781904946502)) published by Discovery Walking Guides Ltd in 2009.

All map sections are aligned so that north is at the top of the page. Waypoint positions, and numbers, refer to the walking route that the map section is illustrating.

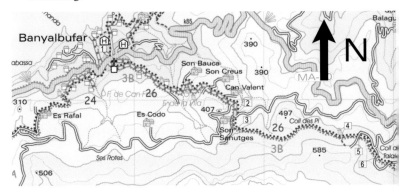

Altitude Profiles

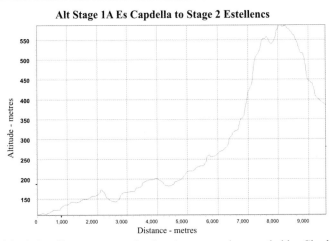

Altitude Profiles are prepared using the gps track, recorded by Charles, for each stage of the GR221 as a plot of Altitude above sea level against distance. Each "Profile" covers the altitude range and distance for that stage so that combined with the map sections you can quickly see the ascents and descents involved in each stage of the GR221.

Port d'Andratx is a small resort but it's getting bigger and, by the looks of things, has aspirations to get bigger still, which is a pity, because until comparatively recently it had a lot going for it. Even now, if you half close your eyes and pretend there's not a small army of villas marching up the hillside, it is still possible to picture the appealing fishing port that developed in the seventeenth century and to appreciate why this sheltered mooring became western Mallorca's main conduit of commerce. The damage being done by property developers notwithstanding, if you take it for what it is (not much, but so it goes) **Port d'Andratx** is a perfectly adequate springboard for our adventure, the more so since it is soon left behind, and we get into wild, untenanted land within half-an-hour of beginning our walk.

Contrasted with its money-gutted neighbour, **Sant Elm** is a thoroughly beguiling place, though to describe it as a 'fishing harbour', which some guidebooks do, is pushing it a bit. There are fishing boats and, judging by the trail of gulls that follow the larger boats back through the **Es Freu** straits, fish are caught, but one glance will tell you that this small community does not support itself by selling a couple of pollack and the odd slab of tuna. Its nucleus in the old fishing hamlets of **S'Algar** and **Cala Conills** is still just discernible, but nowadays it is a small tourist town, the chief attractions of which are its tranquility, and the proximity of two great sites: the abandoned **La Trapa** monastery and the fabulous little dragon-backed isle of **Sa Dragonera**.

La Trapa with Sa Dragonera in the background

The odd bit of graffiti protests against property speculation and calls for an end to building around **Sant Elm**, but looking at the resort from the outside, I suspect that's largely nimbyism because this is one place where the major conservation battles appear to have been won.

There is, for instance, a stretch of kerb threading its way along the coast to the north of **Sant Elm** where someone clearly wanted to build villas and clearly got stopped in the nick of time (the course of the projected road is highly recommended for an evening stroll to watch the sun set over **Dragonera**); and, in one of the most famous cases of environmental militancy on the island, **Dragonera** itself was saved from the property developers by petitions, street protests, and all manner of cheering direct action back in the 1980s.

I'm not really a resort man, but if you've got to have a resort, I'd say somewhere small and discreet and immaculately located like **Sant Elm** is just about perfect. Dear to the Mallorcan sense of self, too, for it was here that King Jaume I first dropped anchor in 1229 when he popped over from Catalunya with a few shiploads of mercenaries intent on grabbing Mallorca back from the Moors.

Apart from hunting down a hotel and setting off from there for a few walks, I haven't spent much time in **S'Arraco** (I only discovered that it had a B&B by chance after we'd left the island, its existence apparently unknown to the Andratx tourism office), but it looks a pleasant place and seems to have constructed itself around the premise that one of everything really ought to be enough for anyone, having one hotel, one B&B, one deli, one restaurant, one baker, pretty much just the one road . . . oh, and three bars, but then some things in life demand multiplication.

Despite its attachment to the singular and its relative seclusion from the rest of the region (the name comes from Arabic ar.rakon which corresponds to Spanish '*rincon*', indicating the interior of a corner or, more familiarly, a remote spot), **S'Arraco** seems to have had a fairly colourful history, long being the resort of bandits, and latterly developing such a strong sense of local identity that there was even an 'independence' movement complete with its own newspaper, La Voz Arraconense, dedicated to an ultimately doomed attempt to maintain autonomy from **Andratx**.

Andratx itself is a pleasant lively little town where expats and locals mix well and easily, conspiring as best they can to keep their agreeable life divorced from that of the holidaymakers and ephemeral visitors. It's almost as if the town council sat down and said, "Right, we've got all these tourists to deal with, what are we going to do with them? I know, let's stick 'em down on the coast and keep the town for us". True, that's where the tourists wanted to be, but at times the separation can seem a little more studied than mere happenstance would explain.

Certainly, **Andratx** doesn't feel like a   town sustained by tourism, the only concessions to foreigners being the availability of British and German newspapers, one German supermarket, and a very helpful lady hidden away in a cubbyhole beside the main entrance to the town hall (it looks a bit like the place where they used to keep the bins) where she has to make shift as a one-woman tourism office.

The partition we first see in **Andratx** of locals settling inland and the coast being left for the 'invaders' is an ancient one. Nowadays, the invasion is of tourists (several million a year for Mallorca as a whole), but in the past it was pirates that compelled the islanders to hide away several kilometres back from the shore, and there's no settlement on the route of the GR221 that does not have its corresponding port, often considerably less developed than the mother town, despite the demands of modern tourism.

Most websites about this area reflect the **Port d'Andratx** ethos and are compendiums of quite stunning banality. Nonetheless, there's a useful tourism section on the town hall's website (www.andratx.net) that would be a bit more useful if it existed in English, too. If you wish to judge for yourself ahead of your trip whether the port is spoiled or not, have a look at the **Port d'Andratx** album on www.travel.webshots.com. **St. Elm** has no dedicated website, but if you google '**Sant Elm**', there are plenty of rental promotions and online guides featuring photos of the place. For more information about **S'Arraco**, including photos old and new, and a distressingly surreal automatic translation, see www.sarraco.org.

Sa Dragonera as seen from La Trapa

Port d'Andratx

Comellar de Can Rodella

Pas Vermell

Sant Elm

Sunset over Dragonera

La Trapa

Dragonera

Mirador Josep Sastre

Stage One, Day One, Dilemma One - a bed. The start of the GR221 explores the rugged countryside surrounding Andratx in the southwest of the island, climbing from **Port d'Andratx** to circle the beautiful wide dry basin of the **Comellars de Can Rodella** and **Cala d'Egos** then crossing the spectacular **Pas Vermell** into the **S'Arraco** valley and descending to the delightful resort of **St. Elm**. Thereafter, a brief but unforgettable ascent brings us to the fabulous setting of a former Trappist monastery and the haven of the refuge. That, at least, is the theory and, insofar as the walking is concerned, it translates into very appealing practice. The trouble is, the **La Trapa** refuge doesn't exist.

For years volunteers have been gathering to work here during the summer and some progress has been made, but like so much else at this end of the *Ruta de Pedra en Sec*, the refuge remains *en proyecto* and is likely to do so for some time to come. Last time we were there we chanced upon a party of journalists with a local politician who wanted to get the scheme going again. The journalists didn't seem convinced. Pressed for an opinion, a particularly laconic photographer launched one of those expansive Mediterranean shrugs that are so eloquent of Latin What-can-one-do-ism, and said, "The money, he keeps disappearing".

It's tempting to suggest they should just leave the place alone. The Trappists always had an eye for promising real estate and **La Trapa** is no exception, an enviably isolated valley perched above plummeting cliffs with breathtaking views over the dominant natural phenomenon at this end of Mallorca, the soaring spine of **Dragonera** island, probably one of the most photographed bits of rock in the Western Mediterranean. The Trappists were only here for fourteen years, caught between bouts of anticlericalism in their native France and in their adopted homeland, but there was nothing short term about their choice of location - this is the sort of place you want to stay.

Unfortunately, you can't! If you're bivouacking out, you could shelter in the outbuildings or the restored mill, but even campers will have second thoughts about stopping here as it would mean carrying enough water for two days. My first idea for finding accommodation was to push on to the **Coll de Sa Gramola** then descend to **Andratx** with a view to taxiing back up the next day, but then I discovered the only hotel in **Andratx** itself is an *agroturismo finca*. They tend to come a bit dear and it seemed a pity to penalize people who are doing the itinerary on a budget. Happily, there is a small hotel and a B&B in the charming little village of **S'Arraco**, so we've gone for that somewhat more democratic option, with the recommendation that you catch the morning L100 bus to **Andratx** (there are three buses between 7.45 and 10.15) then taxi up to the **Pla de s'Evangelica** for Stage Two.

NOTE: If you prefer to stay at the **Andratx** *agroturismo*, see Stage Two for a description of the climb to **Coll de Sa Gramola** and subsequent descent into town.

The full route from **Port d'Andratx** to **S'Arraco** can easily be done in a single day, however the extension does mean it's quite long for the first day of an LDP, so I have broken it into two parts. The first section between **Port d'Andratx** and **Sant Elm** would be ideal for a short walk on the day of arrival. Buses leave **Palma** at forty minutes past the hour and take eighty minutes to reach **Port d'Andratx**.

This stage of the GR is not sign or wayposted. In the unlikely event that a flurry of activity suddenly has signposts sprouting all over the place and they indicate a different route from the one described here, it is advisable to follow the signposted route.

1A Port d'Andratx to St. Elm

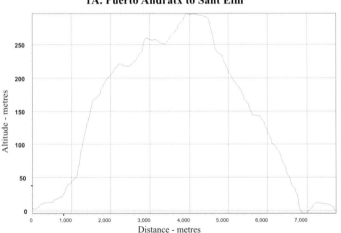

* in Sant Elm

1A. Puerto Andratx to Sant Elm

From the northern end of **Port d'Andratx** marina, we take 'Carretera Aldea Blanca' (Wp.1 0M) then turn left 150 metres later into the 'Carrer de Cala d'Egos' (Wp.2). Forking right at the Y-junction after another 150 metres (Wp.3), we stay on the 'Carrer de Cala d'Egos' and follow the dirt track it leads into. Reaching a metal gate 200

Fan Palm

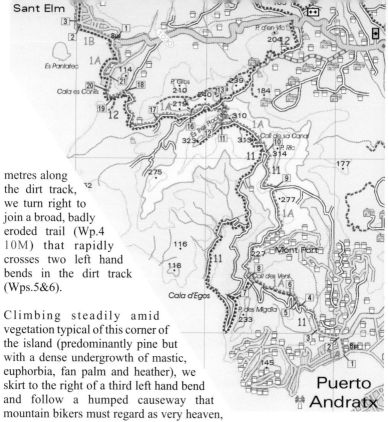

metres along the dirt track, we turn right to join a broad, badly eroded trail (Wp.4 10M) that rapidly crosses two left hand bends in the dirt track (Wps.5&6).

Climbing steadily amid vegetation typical of this corner of the island (predominantly pine but with a dense undergrowth of mastic, euphorbia, fan palm and heather), we skirt to the right of a third left hand bend and follow a humped causeway that mountain bikers must regard as very heaven, always presuming their feet don't slip off the pedals, in which case it would rapidly turn pretty hellish. Toward the top of the humps, we veer left to cross the track beside a large concrete cistern (Wp.7 23M).

Two paths climb beyond the track, one (not very clear from below) directly in front of the cistern, the other more obvious path ten metres to the right. The two paths merge 50 metres later, just short of an intersection of tracks and trails on the **Coll des Vent** (Wp.8 25M), where there are twin limekilns and views open out behind us over **Port d'Andratx** - a lot more attractive from this perspective than when you're actually in it!

Maintaining direction (NNW) to the left of the limekilns, we follow a rough track climbing behind the upper reaches of the Urbanizacíon Mont Port, bringing into view the Llebig lighthouse on the southern tip of **Dragonera** and, on the far side of the valley, a distinctive red-and-white antenna which we will pass just before Wp.11. After passing the last house in the Urbanizacíon

Comellar de Can Rodella

Mont Port, which has a striking stained glass window in its stairwell, we come to a natural *mirador* overlooking the wonderful wild landscape of the **Comellars de Can Rodella** and **Cala d'Egos**, by which time I can pretty well guarantee you'll be well into the walk and will have already forgotten most of your cares.

Ignoring successive shortcuts (all overgrown and largely redundant), we

S'Arraco valley

turn left at a crossroads (Wp.9 47M) then immediately fork left at a Y-junction with a minor track climbing to the right. Coming to a second Y-junction, this time with a track descending to **Cala d'en Egos**, a track that's been intermittently visible since **Coll des Vent**, we fork right (Wp.10 54M) and climb to a ridge overlooking the S'Arraco valley.

Worth pausing here if you intend doing the extension down to **S'Arraco**, which is the village in the middle of the valley. To the left of **S'Arraco** are two summits, the taller one with three peaks. The smaller, more westerly of the two, is the **Puig d'en Guida**, which we circle in Stage 1B Wps.28-32. Just above the pine trees to the left of the *puig*, you should also be able to pick out the white dot of the **Caseta de l'Amo en Pep** ruin (Wp.1B28). In a direct line behind the ruin on the distant ridge, you can see some houses and pine trees, the **Casetas de ses Basses** (Wps.1B20-24). Off to the right, we can see the distinctive triangular summit of **Galatzó** and, to its left, **s'Esclop** or 'the clog' (looking very cloglike from this perspective, albeit an inverted clog showing the heel and flat of the sole), which we traverse in Stage Two.

125 metres after passing to the left of the red and white antenna seen earlier, we leave the dirt track, turning right at a large cairn (Wp.11 65M) onto a rough path that immediately disappears amid bulges of exposed limestone. Following the cairns, we climb to the first pass of the our itinerary, the **Pas Vermell** (Wp.12 67M), a narrow crossing in the rock leading to a long broad ledge of reddish rock running alongside the

red rock of Pas Vermell

Dragonera from Wp.12

overhang of the antenna summit. Below us we can see a green fire fighting reservoir, where we join a track climbing from **S'Arraco** (an alternative way to the Hotel s'Escaleta, but a bit pointless since it skips all the bits that make this stage most interesting). We also see **St. Elm** and get our first uninterrupted view of **Dragonera**.

Forestry Cabin after Wp.17

After the ledge of reddish rock, we descend rapidly on a narrow path toward the fire-fighting reservoir, 75 metres short of which the path divides, an old, eroded stretch dropping down to the right (Wp.13 74M). We stay on the main path to join the dirt track directly in front of the fire-fighting reservoir at the **Coll de sa Barrera** (Wp.14).

Maintaining direction (SW), we follow the track, taking advantage of a shortcut after the first bend (Wp.15 77M). Ignoring a branch off to the left (Wp.16 80M), we descend through dense woodland with more oleaster among the pine than in the woods above **Port d'Andratx**. At the bottom of a second cairn-marked shortcut, when the path rejoins the main track (Wp.17 86M), we turn right on a broad trail that soon becomes a car track. The track passes an attractive forestry cabin, below which we swing round towards **Na Pòpia**, the highest summit on **Dragonera**, passing a '*Camino Privado*' sign forbidding vehicles.

St. Elm soon comes into view and the track goes through a chained gateway to reach a broad parking area where it veers sharp right (Wp.18 92M). We leave the track at this point, turning left on a broad path running along the southern flank of a gully, apparently taking us away from **St. Elm**. However, forking right 100 metres later (Wp.19), we follow a faint, cairn-marked path (I suspect the GR will eventually choose a more commodious route into **St. Elm**, but this one is the most attractive) descending toward a small block of flats. Shadowing the fence to the left of the flats then crossing the band of rock in front of them, we clamber onto the steps behind **Cala es Conills** (Wp.20). We now follow the road into **St. Elm**, turning left at the 'S'Arraco, Andratx, Palma' sign (Wp.21) to reach the bus stop behind the **Cala en Gemec** beach.

3	3½ H	11.3 km	↗ 500m ↘ 420m	⟷	4*

* at S'Arraco

1B. Sant Elm to La Trapa

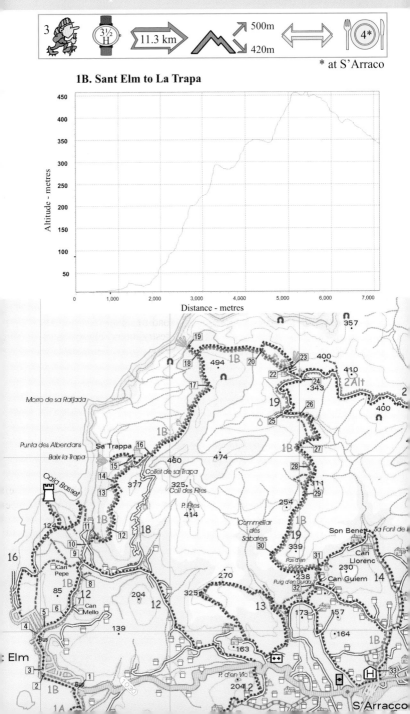

From the bus stop behind the **Cala en Gemec** beach (Wp.1 0M), we walk up **St. Elm's** main pedestrianized street, passing the Hostal Dragonera. At the end of the pedestrianized stretch (Wp.2 5M), we carry straight on then bear left at the roundabout into 'Carrer Cala en Basset' (Wp.3). The road swings right at the junction with 'Carrer des Carregador' to pass the 'Es Moli' restaurant in the 'Plaza de Mossén Sebastia Grau' from where we take 'Avinguda de la Trapa' (Wp.4) carrying straight on 75 metres later on the same *avinguda* when the main road swings left (Wp.5). When the tarmac ends 200 metres later, we continue on the 'Cami de Can Tomevi' dirt track (Wp.6 16M).

Ignoring a branch doubling back to the right (Wp.7) and a broad path forking off to the right (Wp.8 23M), we follow the Cami de Can Tomevi as it meanders through pleasant pine wood, beyond which we can glimpse the crags below which we climb to **La Trapa**. At the derelict, bricked up remains of **Can Tomevi** (the house with a faintly bamboozled looking bull daubed on its wall) (Wp.9 26M), we leave the track, ignoring signposted routes to 'La Trapa' on the right and 'Sa Torre' on the left (the *torre* in question being the martello tower above **Cala en Basset**), instead carrying straight on along a broad cairn-marked trail currently signposted 'Cala emBasset' (sic).

Climbing gently, we cross a dirt track beside a couple of gateposts (Wp.10 29M). Thereafter, the trail divides briefly and the climb steepens as we veer right at a roofless ruin (Wp.11 33M), passing (on our left 50 metres later) our first *sitja*. The path is slightly obscure here, but it's easily followed due to the cairns every 10 metres, and it soon becomes a clear trail traversing the face of the crags seen earlier.

The path between Wps.11 & 12

Cala d'en Basset from Wp.12

After crossing a small anonymous pass overlooking **Cala d'en Basset** (Wp.12 44M), we maintain a northerly direction along the flank of the crags, traversing a shoulder within sight of the last very rocky pass into the **Vall de Sant Josep**, where **La Trapa** is located. An easy approach to the foot of the pass (Wp.13

Approaching Wp.13

56M) leads into a waymarked route climbing through and occasionally directly over the rocks onto the high ground overlooking **La Trapa** (Wp.14 61M), from where a gentle descent brings us to the main track directly above the wannabe refuge (Wp.15 68M). Whatever the state of the place, it's well worth taking a break here. For a picnic spot, it's hard

terraces above La Trapa

to beat the threshing circle overlooking **Dragonera**.

Returning to Wp.15, we climb along the main track for 300 metres, ignoring three branch tracks onto terraces on our left. At the second sharp right hand bend, we leave the track, turning left onto a narrow path and ignoring the sign that indicates an alternative route to **S'Arraco** along the track (Wp.16 76M). The narrow path winds through the scrub alongside the upper reaches of the **Vall de Sant Josep**. Our next objective, the **Mirador d'en Josep Sastre**, is up to the left, at the end of a long line of scrub covered rock.

The path contours round abandoned terraces, climbing occasionally, gently at first then more steeply, to cross an affluent of the **Serral Llarg** watercourse, 125 metres after which, directly behind the main watercourse, we bear left at an intersection of paths (Wp.17 95M) to reach a second junction beside a very large pile of stones (Wp.18 101M). 100 metres to the left lies the most toe-curling *mirador* I ever hope to encounter, the **Mirador d'en Josep Sastre** (Wp.19), perched on top of the **Cap Fabioler** cliffs, 450 very direct metres above the sea. The perspective on **Dragonera** is extraordinary. So is the nausea.

cliffs below Carregador

Once you've overcome your dizzy spell and have stopped staggering about gasping with delighted horror, retrace your steps to the large pile of stones and bear left to follow the path as it contours round the **Ses Basses** heights. The gasping is not over yet, though, because equally splendid views soon open out toward the beautiful cliffs below **Punta Carregador** and **Penyals s'Evangelica**, and up toward the distinctive clog of **s'Esclop**, which is where we're heading in Stage Two.

Forking right at a Y-junction (Wp.20 114M), we join the end of a dirt track, along which we descend, passing the **Casetas de ses Basses**. We stay on the main track, ignoring two paths forking off to the left, the second of which is waymarked (Wps.21 & 22), and a branch track off to the left (Wp.23). At a junction of tracks 150 metres after passing the entrance to a *caseta* on the right, we leave the projected route of the GR, doubling back to the right to pass below the *caseta* (Wp.24 125M). This is where the **S'Arraco** extension begins. If you're not descending to the hotel, bear left at this junction and skip to the Stage Two description.

1B. Extension wpt 24 to S'Arraco

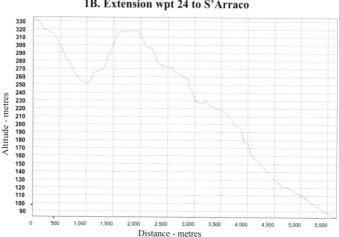

The **S'Arraco** track descends steadily into a dramatic, desiccated, austere landscape, passing a branch climbing to the right (Wp.25). 200 metres later, our track peters out above a dam wall (Wp.26 138M) and we continue on a path, clearly visible throughout the descent. The path climbs gently along the right bank of the **Torrent Gore d'en Betts** (AKA Torrent de sa Font), then veers round to the right, climbing through a

Caseta de l'Amo en Pep Wp.28

series of long chicanes to join another trail running along a retaining wall (Wp.27 148M).

This trail soon veers round (SE) to cross a small plateau and drop down to a ruined cabin, the **Caseta de l'Amo en Pep** (Wp.28 154M). Beyond the ruin, the path descends across rough ground to a stand of pine (Wp.29 161M) where progress becomes smoother underfoot. Skirting to the left of a terraced valley, the **Rotes de s'Hereu** (a *rota* being a mountain smallholding with a cabin), we cross a rocky pass (Wp.30 171M), after which our path broadens to a trail.

Passing between the **Puig d'en Guida** and the **Puig d'en Corsó**, we descend to a Y-junction (Wp.31 182M), where we turn right, as indicated by red waymarks, descending past the small house of **Can Corsó**. 75 metres later, the waymarked path forks off to the right (Wp.32 187M), eventually emerging near the local sports field and the MA-1030 bus-stop. However, for simplicity's sake and to arrive directly at our accommodation, we stay on the dirt track and the newly asphalted lane it leads into, and follow it all the way into **S'Arraco** where it becomes 'Calle del Porvenir', on which you will find the Hotel d'Escaleta (Wp.33 217M).

Given the accommodation detour at the end of Stage One and the somewhat provisional nature of Stage Two (rights-of-way yet to be confirmed, scant waymarking, and a brief stretch of very tricky pathfinding), it seemed only fair to offer an alternative start to the GR221 for those who don't mind missing the (admittedly considerable) attractions of the official Stage One. Taking advantage of the recently purchased **Finca Publica Galatzó** and the even more recently cleared *Cami de ses Sinies* dirt track penetrating the valley behind the *finca*, we climb into the wild, pathless, untenanted terrain between the west's two iconic mountains, **S'Esclop** and **Galatzó**, then descend via the dramatic **Pas des Cossis** and the **Boal de ses Serveres** picnic area to join the conventional end of Stage Two.

Apart from the *finca* itself, there is no single natural or monumental feature en route that makes this a must-do path, but it's an excellent introduction to the sort of desiccated, slightly haunting landscape that predominates at the two extremes of the **Tramuntana**, and a crash course in the Mallorcan plant par excellence, *carritx* or diss grass. There is a long section that is effectively off-path, but a profusion of cairns mean pathfinding is not a problem. That said, some care is required in identifying Wp.12.

The only drawback is that there is no accommodation in **Es Capdella** itself, so doing this alternative would mean staying overnight in Palma and catching the morning bus (9.20), which reaches **Es Capdella** at 10.40. Those of you bivouacking out will be interested to note that there are a number of restored charcoal burners' huts en route. I don't doubt they were restored for purposes of anthropological edification rather than nomadic accommodation and that sleeping out in them is formally prohibited, but even so . . . interesting to note!

3 — 2½ H* — 8¾ km — 480m / 450m — 4**

* to Stage 2 Wp.30   ** in Estellencs

Alt Stage 1A Es Capdella to Stage 2 Estellencs

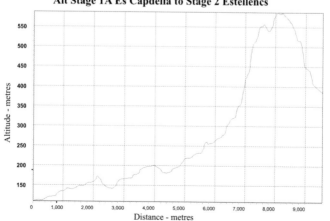

Galatzó lane

From the central crossroads in **Es Capdella**, directly opposite the *ayuntamiento*, we take 'Carrer de Galatzó', which is also signposted 'Finca Publica Galatzó' (Wp.1 0M). The road soon leaves the village, becoming an attractive country lane that passes the 'Cami del Graner Delme' dirt track after 450 metres (Wp.2). Ignoring all branches, we now simply follow this lane and its continuation as a dirt track (N) traversing extensive groves of almond and carob trees until it reaches the gates of the *finca publica* a kilometre-and-a-half later, enjoying throughout fine views of the distinctive pyramid of **Galatzó** itself, and taking advantage of the level ground that really let's us get into our stride.

150 metres after the estate gates, we ignore a fork off to the left for 'Sa Vinya' (Wp.3 31M), and continue on the main track toward the farmhouse, which is clearly visible in the distance. At a slanting T-junction with another track, we bear left (Wp.4 39M), passing another 'Sa Vinya' path 90 metres later, where we stay on the main track to reach the farmhouse, which has a magnificent facade studded with small stones (Wp.5 45M) - no, it's not just pebble dash!

Carrying straight on underneath a high balcony (unless otherwise directed: at the time of writing, there's a temporary detour doglegging round the house via the stables at its western end), we follow a bridleway between walls, where we see the first of the orange tipped fencing-posts that waymark various routes round the hinterland of the estate. The bridleway soon broadens to a dirt track again, on which we maintain a northerly direction through the remaining cultivated land of the estate, approaching the **Comellar de ses Sinies**, a wooded valley that appears to be blocked at the far end by an impassable wall of scrub clad rock.

At a signposted junction with a branch off to the left for the 'Font de sa Cometa', we fork right for 'Pou de ses Sinies' (Wp.6 52M), staying on the main track, which soon dips down, passing what will be for many of you your first limekilns. Continuing amid classic vegetation for this end of the island (*carritx*, dwarf palm, pine, and the odd oleaster making a poor fist of survival among the rocks), we can also expect to see our first wild goats. The terrain becomes wilder as we near the upper reaches of the valley, bringing into view several natural breaches in what had previously seemed a solid wall of rock sealing the valley off.

Toward the head of the valley, we pass a couple of picnic tables beside a cluster of thatched charcoal burners' cabins and the earth covered reconstitution of a charcoal oven or *sitja*, the circular scars of which are abundant throughout the woods of **Mallorca**. 75 metres later, we come to

Wp.7

the **Pou** (or well) **de ses Sinies** at a signposted junction, where we leave the main track and turn right on a minor track for 'S'Esclop' (Wp.7 73M). Gird up your loins and any other girdable bits you've got about you, because the easy strolling we've enjoyed so far is finished.

Ignoring a path climbing to a small ruin (the 'Naveta de ses Sinies') on the left 175 metres later, we pass the first of the new smaller wayposts topped with a purple band that guide us for the better part of our climb out of the valley (and thereafter up to Wp.27 of Stage Two if the refuge has opened and you intend staying there), in this instance indicating that we fork left at a Y-junction (Wp.8 77M). The track narrows to a trail here and the climbing begins, gradually at first then more steeply, tracing a couple of long traverses across the *carritx* covered slope at the mouth of the more westerly of the two dry torrents feeding into the **Comellar de ses Sinies**.

approaching the
starburst of torrents

Ignoring an old pink arrow indicating a path on the left now swallowed up by the vegetation (Wp.9 82M), we carry straight on, following the obvious trail. After a steady to steep climb, some of it on roughly cobbled trail, we cross the first of two stone clad *sitjes*

(Wp.10 92M). The steady climb continues into increasingly wild terrain as what had appeared to be one homogenous watercourse splinters into a starburst of affluent torrents. Favouring the eastern flank of the valley, we continue climbing steadily to steeply, eventually crossing the course of the old torrent and passing a second stone clad *sitja* (Wp.11 107M).

50 metres short of the crags at the head of the valley, we reach a junction of paths (Wp.12 112M). The clear, purple wayposted route climbs to the west to join Stage Two at Wp.27 above the **Coma d'en Vidal** refuge. We, however, turn right on a path that is initially invisible, swamped as it is by *carritx*, but which is clearly marked by a cairn and bright red dot. As we head east, leaving the main valley behind us and bringing **Galatzó** back into view, the path broadens, contouring round the hillside above one of the affluent torrents, then disappears in the rock below a large pine (Wp.13 115M)

The unmistakable rise of **Galatzó** lies off to our right. At the foot **Galatzó** on its northern side is **Sa Moleta Rasa**, a small summit clad with pine on its eastern face. Immediately to the left of **Sa Moleta Rasa** is an elevated band of rock topped by two pine. Our ongoing route passes to the left of the two-pine-topped rock (TPTR). The 'path', such as it is, is never visible for more than a few metres ahead, but is generally clear step-by-step, and

Carritx & Cairns

is peppered with so many cairns you'd have to make a concerted effort to get lost.

Taking care to follow the cairns, we pick our way (NE) through the *carritx,* a bit of a baptism of fire if you're unfamiliar with this most abundant of Mallorcan plants. The key thing to know about *carritx* is that it has an uncanny knack for insinuating its draping tips under the boot of your forward foot so that the following foot snags on the trapped fronds and the unwary walker goes sprawling.

Climbing to cross the rocks immediately west of the TPTR, we come to a large cairn beside two other pine within sight of the sea (Wp.14 125M). Ignoring cairns off to the left (they trace out an alternative route to Wp.27 of Stage Two), we follow the more obvious and larger cairns (NE), passing behind the TPTR to another large cairn on bare rock (Wp.15 128M). The way is slightly more obscure here, but maintaining direction (NE) we soon see more cairns leading to a broad col marked with a 'Big Game Hunting' warning sign, from where we have sweeping sea views (Wp.16 133M).

On our right, there's a cairn marked way heading due east to **Galatzó**, but we carry straight on, descending past the 'big game' (it's goats they're talking about) sign toward the sea. The path is increasingly clear now, but the cairns still help distinguish its course amid the *carritx* and a scattering of replanted pine. We're apparently heading for a sheer drop here, but a couple of hundred metres later, the path swings right to reach a signposted junction with the main northern approach to **Galatzó**, directly above the **Pas des Cossis** (Wp.17 139M).

Wp.16

Big Game

Turning left for 'Boal de ses Serveres', we take a clear path down through the pass, still apparently heading for a sheer drop, but in fact following a well graded way winding down the steep slope to the pine and Holm Oak wood, beyond which we come to the **Boal de ses Serveres** picnic area, where there's another restored charcoal burners' hut (restored some years ago - the 'roof' wouldn't keep out anything very elemental), a chemical loo, picnic tables and barbecues, but not water. Turning left on the dirt track crossing the picnic area (Wp.18 148M), we descend to join Stage Two beside a green fire-fighting reservoir at Wp.30 (153M) a little under an hour from **Estellencs**.

Many of the old Royal Ways of Spain have been obliterated by dirt tracks and new roads, but if there's one thing **Mallorca** doesn't lack, it's twisting, turning, spiralling, dizzying switchback roads, and despite the fact that it's the most direct route between **Puigpunyent** and **Estellencs**, nobody seems to have thought that it would be a good idea to asphalt the *Camí Real* or *Camí Vell d'Estellencs*, for which we can be grateful, since the oversight has preserved some very agreeable walking country.

The state of the cobbling on the *camí* is poor by Mallorcan standards and was apparently already regarded as lamentable in the early nineteenth century, its degradation blamed on the foraging of pigs from the **Son Fortesa** estate. Since then, forestry tracks and the installation of power pylons have done more damage to the ancient metalling, but for all that, it is still an attractive alternative way onto the GR221, crossing some lovely woodland with fine sea views, and passing two of the most impressive manor houses in the west, **Son Fortesa** and **Son Fortuny**.

Like Alternative Start 1A via **Es Capdella**, this option is designed for those who don't want to deal with the accommodation hassles of Stage One or the provisional nature of Stage Two, but still fancy an extra day's walking rather than simply beginning the path at **Banyalbufar**. If you want wilderness and open vistas, the **Es Capdella** alternative is recommended. If hot weather is likely, the shadier **Puigpunyent** alternative is preferable. As with Stages 1A and 3B, the *Camí Vell d'Estellencs* would be suitable for a short walk on the first day. The morning buses leave Palma at 9.05 and 11.30, arriving half an hour later.

Man's impact on the landscape is particularly marked hereabouts and there are so many instersections that reading the route you might begin to suspect you're in the middle of a wiring diagram. However, pathfinding is not generally a problem. All major intersections of the ascent are clearly marked, either with signposts, wayposts, or cairns. The descent is more sketchily waymarked, but poses no problems until it bottoms out beside the **Torrent des Aigua** below the **Son Fortuny** manor house, where some care is required to follow the described itinerary.

* in Estellencs

Our itinerary starts at kilometre 1 of the MA-1101. To reach the start from the 'Cantonada Escola' bus stop in the centre of **Puigpunyent**, head uphill, past the 'Restaurant ses Cotxeries', bearing left after 600 metres on the 'Carretera Nova d'Estellencs'. The kilometre post is at a Y-junction 200 metres later (Wp.1 0M).

While the MA-1101 swings right behind the km1 marker, we fork left and carry straight on through the gate 75 metres later, where there are signs

Alt1B Puigpuyent to Estellencs

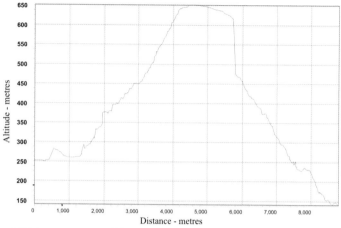

prohibiting cars, motorbikes and cyclists. We follow this lane, which is particularly lovely in spring, toward the peak of **Galatzó** poking over the treetops. After a little over a kilometre, the lane climbs alongside the high, eastern wall of the **Son Fortesa** manor house, then swings left to approach the house from the northeast, at which point a waypost marks two tracks off to our right (Wp.2 14M).

The clearer track with black gates goes through the **Son Fortesa**

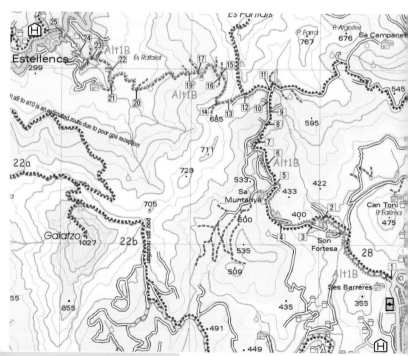

farmyard, but we take the nearer and narrower of the two tracks, which has a rusty gate and a sign for the 'Camí Vell d'Estellencs'. After going through a bedstead gate, we rejoin the main track (Wp.3 23M) and turn right, beginning our steady climb. When the track veers sharp right beside a large boulder that has broken away from the embankment, we carry straight on, following a wayposted shortcut (Wp.4 31M) that rejoins the main track 100 metres later, within sight of the abandoned **Sa Muntanya** farmhouse - worth crossing the track here to check out the small ruin off to our right, which has been pieced together (it does rather resemble a jigsaw puzzle) with stone and some wonderful homemade bricks.

the Son Fortesa lane

home made bricks

We continue along the track, climbing gently past a small spring below

The Sa Muntanya Spring

the old farmhouse, to the northeast of which the track swings sharp left to a junction, where we bear right, staying on the main track as it enters the woods that are such a feature of the **Tramuntana** (Wp.5 41M). Forking left at the next Y-junction (Wp.6 45M), we climb steadily on a narrow track that eventually goes through a gateway in a wall, 20 metres after which, when the track doubles back to the left, we carry straight on along a broad walking trail (Wp.7 49M).

The steady climb continues, occasionally on sections of cobbling, but mainly on a carpet of Holm Oak leaf mulch, crossing another track then rejoining it 50 metres later (Wp.8 54M). Bearing right, we climb to an intersection with the bend of another track (Wp.9 58M), at which point we carry straight on (the left hand branch), still climbing and ignoring an overgrown branch off to the left 75 metres later (Wp.10). Eventually we come to a signposted junction indicating that 'Es Grau', the *coll* on the road midway between **Puigpunyent** and **Esporles**, is down to our right. Leaving the wayposted route, we turn left to continue climbing steadily through the woods (Wp.11 62M).

The track levels out 250 metres later and we traverse a heavily wooded plateau, passing a waymarked path branching off to the right (Wp.12 69M) (nothing you want to be doing while encumbered by a bulky backpack) and a faint spur off to the left, 75 metres after which we reach the **Coll d'Estellencs** (Wp.13 71M), where there's a wall with a

**Galatzó & S'Esclop
from Puntal de Planicia**

locked gate and a stile, the latter disabled by a bad case of foot rot, but still sturdy enough to be used.

Ignoring a cairn-marked branch off to the left 150 metres after the wall (Wp.14 74M), we fork left 250 metres later (Wp.15 78M) then turn right after another 50 metres (Wp.16), as indicated by the cairns and old red waymarks that guide us (intermittently it must be said) down the northern side of the mountain. There's a real maze of tracks and trails and paths throughout this descent, as if somebody's sketched out a double helix on the side of the mountain just to confuse hapless mapmakers, but as long as you bear in mind that we're going down all the way and don't get beguiled onto one of the red-herring routes helpfully traced out by sheep on the lower terraces, the route is reasonably clear.

After going through a gate in a new fence, we descend to a curlicue T-junction, where we turn left as indicated by a green arrow painted on a rock (Wp.17 86M). Thereafter, patches of the old cobbled trail become more evident as our path weaves back and forth alongside and occasionally crossing the dry bed of the **Torrent de Son Jover**. Turning right at a second T-junction (Wp.18 90M), we descend to an intersection with a dirt track (Wp.19 92M), where we bear left to continue our descent.

Son Fortuny

Track and torrent diverge as we enter an increasingly domestic landscape and get glimpses of the magnificent **Son Fortuny** manor house. When the track swings sharp right (Wp.20 104M), we turn left on a cobbled trail between two walls, as indicated by three clear red dots on a rock. Track and trail soon converge and we continue winding back and forth across abandoned olive terraces as we approach the terraced, cultivated valley of the **Torrent des Aigua** (AKA Torrent Major), which separates us from **Son Fortuny**. At this point, you'll probably have to consult the book again if you don't want to stray off path.

At a slanting T-junction a couple of hundred metres short of the manor house (Wp.21 115M), we double back to the right, approaching a gate accessing the **Torrent des Aigua** terraces. Instead of going through the gate though, we continue along a broad trail between a retaining wall and a fence to reach a tiny cabin with a red dot on the crumbling retaining wall behind it (Wp.22 119M).

Without climbing onto the terraces, we pass directly behind the cabin on an obscure path that swings round to the right after a few metres to cross the bed of the **Torrent de Son Jover** and go through a gate. We then follow a very rough path alongside the remains of a retaining wall above the right bank of the torrent and go through a second gate, 50 metres after which we cross a restored aquifer and descend onto a surfaced track (Wp.23 124M).

Turning left, we cross a bridge over the **Torrent Major** and join a dirt track linking **Son Fortuny** and the village (Wp.24 128M). Carrying straight on, we simply follow this track to the **Son Fortuny** gates, beyond which we emerge on the MA-10 at the eastern end of **Estellencs** and the notional start of Stage Three (Wp.25). The bus-stop for **Banyalbufar** is at the other end of the village after the Hotel Maristel.

sculpture by Mario Navares

The Colours They Make
- Mallorcan Flora

Speaking as a man who, in a previous publication, confidently described a path as being studded with tiny begonias only to have a reader point out that my 'tiny begonias' were in fact cyclamens, I might be better advised to steer clear of rhapsodies about Mallorcan flora. The thing is though, I might not know much about wildflowers, but I *do* like the colours they make, and it would be a serious oversight in a book of this nature not to tell flower lovers that they're in for a treat.

People who know better than me will tell you that the colours I'm so fond of come from shrubs and flowers like rosemary, broom, St. John's wort, asphodels, rock roses, spurge, myrtle, thyme, crocus, cyclamen (*cyclamen balearicum* to be precise), Friar's cowl, various arums, orchids, foxglove, hellebore, windflowers, blue tobacco . . . and on! There are also plenty of wild fungi, which the Mallorcans gather with a passion I would gladly emulate were it not for the fact that my indomitable ignorance means I'd probably poison myself.

I'm marginally more confident in identifying *carritx*, the diss grass that carpets the island and dangles over paths in a perfectly laid trap for tripping up unwary walkers. As for trees, you can expect extraordinary splashes of colour from mimosa, jacaranda and Judas trees, a gorgeous spectacle when the almond trees are in blossom, and mountains clad in pine, Holm Oak, oleaster and olive.

In many ways, the olive tree is the defining feature of the island's flora, not because it is more abundant than other common trees, but because nowhere else have I seen so many very ancient olive trees. Some

sources say individual trees have been carbon dated to before the birth of Christ, a claim that sounds fantastical until you see the phantasmagoric shapes the trees have been twisted into, so tormented and gnarled that a couple of millennia's exposure to wind, sun, pollarding, and shaking and beating (the last two being the traditional methods for 'picking' olives) seems the only plausible explanation for their beleaguered aspect.

As for the fruit of these venerable monsters, all I can say is that, having lived in various corners of Spain for a dozen years, and what's more having grown and cured my own olives, I have never eaten any as rich and flavoursome as the small, black olives of Mallorca preserved in their own oil. **But then Mallorca's like that: the oranges are more orangey** than elsewhere, the olives more olivey, as if the island's long and troubled history has leant a piquancy to its products that cannot be found elsewhere.

Esclop from near the mirador

Pla de sa Evangelica

pathless terrain

human activity in improbable places

botador at waypoint 11

S'Esclop from the East

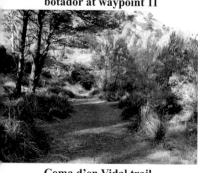
Coma d'en Vidal trail

the refuge

In many ways, Stage Two of the GR221 is the most challenging, in large measure because the precise route it will follow has yet to be confirmed. Look at the *Ruta de Pedra en Sec* sketch map on the *Consell de Mallorca* website and it would appear that we are due to spend the day trudging along the road, dodging the odd car and making Brrrm! Brrrm! noises to break the monotony. Other maps suggest the *Carretera Vella de Estellencs* (an attractive dirt track) between kilometres 102 and 99.7 of the MA-10 is a stretch of the GR. Some even go so far as to show paths climbing from the eastern end of the *Carretera Vella* to the **Coma d'en Vidal** refuge, the projected staging post here, fully restored since 2007, but as yet unopened. These paths don't exist. To be fair, when asked about it, the *Medioamabiente* people say that something along these lines is *'en proyecto'*, but *'en proyecto'* can mean pretty much anything you want it to mean at the western end of the GR221 and, given the rate of progress to date, I wouldn't envisage any great developments in the foreseeable future.

The other option, the one we've chosen, is to climb the **Mola de s'Esclop** ('the clog') via the **Coma des Cellers** and **Ses Alquerioles** estate, then contour round the summit to reach the **Coll de Font des Quer**, from where we have a straightforward descent to the refuge and **Estellencs** via well-established walking routes. However, we are not yet done with the challenges because this option is also *'en proyecto'*, in this instance meaning two things.

First, the rights-of-way are still under negotiation. Local walkers use this ascent regularly and I did it without any problems, but at least half the route is on private property and, in one case near the start, we pass directly in front of a house on a track that is effectively somebody's front yard. There is a risk, slight in my estimation but still extant, that you will be turned back.

Second, pathfinding is very, very difficult, mainly because there are no paths on most of the route. Hopefully my researches will have solved that problem for you (I got lost twice working it out on little more than a wing and prayer), but even so, you should be aware that you are venturing into rough, pathless terrain. For this reason, Stage Two should not be undertaken during poor conditions and is really only recommended for people who know the island reasonably well.

"So what on earth are we doing up here?" you may ask yourself, to which the reply is simple: we're responding to the call of the wild. Although you will see vestiges of human activity, often in highly improbable places, this is undoubtedly the wildest walking on the *Ruta de Pedra en Sec*, taking us into Mallorca's untamed highlands and giving us an idea of just why generations of dedicated walkers have been so passionate about this place. The challenges are not to be underrated, but neither are the rewards.

Due to the accommodation problems (**La Trapa** yet to be built, **Coma d'en Vidal** yet to be opened) our main itinerary for Stage Two starts and ends a little later than the official version. The **Ses Basses** to **Pla de s'Evangèlica** link (for those of you camping) and the descent to **Andratx** from **Coll de Sa Gramola** (for those who opt to stay there at the end of Stage One) are also described below. The **Ses Basses** to **Pla de s'Evangèlica** link, **Andratx** descent, and the main stretch of Stage Two between the **Pla de s'Evangèlica** and **Estellencs** are in three separate GPS files. Those of you taxiing up to **Pla de s'Evangèlica** from **Andratx** should skip to page 56.

2 Ses Basses to Pla de s'Evangèlica link

I doubt many people will be walking this first stretch of our Stage Two, not at least until the **La Trapa** refuge is complete, but in case you're camping, or if you wish to stay at **Andratx** rather than **S'Arraco**, here is a description of the approach to **Pla de s'Evangèlica**.

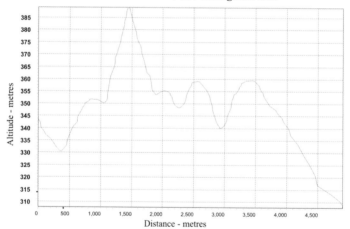

2 Alt Ses Basses to Pla de s'Evangèlica link

At the **S'Arraco** turn-off (Wp.1 0M - Wp.24 of Stage 1B), we carry straight on along the main track and simply follow this track all the way to the MA-10 at **Coll de sa Gramola**. Ignoring two cairn-marked ways climbing to the left in the first kilometre (Wp.2 6M & Wp.3 14M), we stick with the track as it climbs a small rise, from where we have a clear view of **S'Esclop**, 'the clog', with its inverted heel on the right and the sole on the left. Below the 'sole', you should be able to pick out a large green splash of plastic amid the trees behind the **Ses Alquerioles** farm. Our

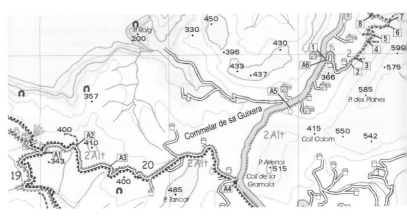

route climbs to the left of this then passes the toe of the clog.

After ignoring a couple of branch tracks and passing a small yellow house, we round a bend, bringing into view the MA-10 and the **Coll de sa Gramola** parking area. Below the road lies a scruffy, fire ravaged valley, the **Commellar de sa Guixeria**. The GR is meant to descend along this valley to avoid most of the road walking, emerging

the 'Clog'

at the **Pla de s'Evangèlica** near km105 of the MA-10, a little over 500 metres from Wp.6. One glance should be enough to tell you this is *'en proyecto'*! The trail down the valley, if ever there was one, is badly overgrown. I believe it is meant to begin at the gates of the last house on the track (House No.7). If there's any sign of the path by the time you arrive, please let us know. For the present though, we stay on the track till it emerges on the road at **Coll de sa Gramola** (Wp.4 42M).

Immediately on the right is the dirt track descending to **Andratx**. To continue on the GR, we turn left, reaching the **Pla de s'Evangèlica** and the putative exit of the *en proyecto* path a kilometre later (Wp.5). At the far end of the *pla*, immediately after the km104.4 metre stone, we take the asphalted lane climbing to the right, signposted 'Sa Coma de ses Selles' (Wp.6).

If you have chosen to stay in **Andratx** rather than **S'Arraco**, here is a brief description of the descent from the **Coll de sa Gramola**. The itinerary was walked in the opposite direction for a previous publication and the present description is simply a reversal of the earlier directions, but the route is very straightforward and should not pose any problems. It should take a little over an hour to reach the **Son Esteve** *agroturismo*. Since this is an alternative to our preferred ending on Stage One, the waypoint numbers carry an 'A1' prefix to indicate its alternative status.

At the **Coll de sa Gramola** (Wp.A101), we turn right and take the track descending southeast alongside the MA-10. At an intersection with a bend on the *Camí de sa Coma Freda* (Wp.A102), we again turn right, ignoring a lane descending on the right (to properties # 39 & 41) 75 metres later. We now simply follow the *Camí de sa Coma Freda* all the way into **Andratx**, carrying straight on at two inverted Y-junctions with the *Camís des Torrent des Pont* and *Son Avidal* (Wps. A103 & A104).

The *Camí de sa Coma Freda* eventually becomes 'Carrer de Barcelona' which ends at a T-junction on the outskirts of **Andratx** (Wp.A105). The shopping area and town centre are off to our left, but to go directly to **Son Esteve**, we turn right, then left 75 metres later into 'Carrer Cuba' (Wp.A106). Carrying straight on at the junction with 'Carrer Catalunya' and 'Carrer Andalucia' (Wp.A107), we follow 'Carrer Galicia' for 750 metres until it comes to a roundabout (Wp.A108), on the far side of which you should be able to see a sign for 'Son Esteve'. Following a narrow lane round to the east, we turn right under a by-pass (Wp.A109) to reach **Son Esteve** 100 metres later (Wp.A110).

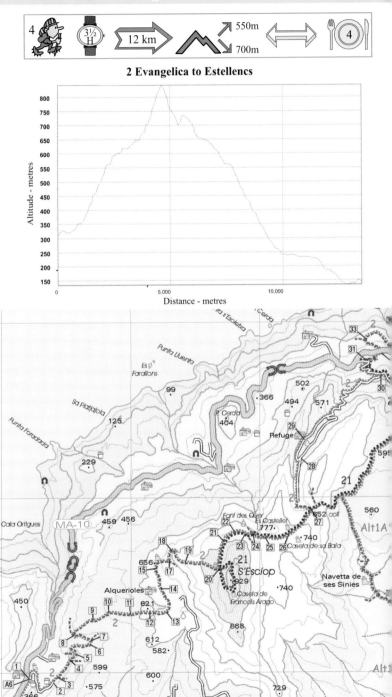

2 Evangelica to Estellencs

From the northern end of the **Pla de s'Evangèlica** , immediately after the km104.4 metre stone, we take the asphalted lane climbing to the right, signposted 'Sa Coma de ses Selles' (Wp.1 0M). A little over 100 metres later, the asphalt gives way to dirt, and 75 metres after that, we pass directly in front of a house, and possibly in front of a loud, faintly mad looking dog on a chain. He actually gets quite playful when you talk to him, but it's probably best to stay at arm's length. 200 metres later, the main track doubles back to the left in front of two gates (Wp.2 8M) to enter a second house. We carry straight on from the bend, going through the left hand gate. Bearing right immediately after the gate to reach a Y-junction (Wp.3), we fork left to contour behind the cabin of the *rota* we've just entered (E then NE).

Ignoring tracks climbing to the right (Wp.4) and descending to the left (Wp.5 13M) (the latter potentially an alternative access to this ascent, starting at km104 of the MA-10), we climb steadily along the **Coma des Cellers**, which, after the desiccated land around **La Trapa**, has a decidedly humid, almost alpine feel to it, especially early on a winter's morning. Eventually, the track veers left through a gateway to reach the ruined **Caseta des Carabinero**. At the point where the track veers left, directly ahead of us there is an old green post (and possibly the remains of a green, bullet-riddled sign lying on the ground). Between the post and the *caseta*, a cairn marks a rough, narrow, reddish way (Wp.6 20M) climbing behind the **Caseta des Carabinero** (N then NW).

The way is obscure, but aiming for the obvious pass in the cliffs off to our left, we fork left after 50 metres (Wp.7) and climb through the scrub on an improving path, soon going through a gateway in a broken down fence. 50 metres after the gateway, we reach a large, solitary black pine at the top of the pass, known as **Pas Gran** (Wp.8 27M), from where we have fine views over the **Pla de s'Evangèlica**. We now begin our first long off-path stretch.

Bearing right and following a clearly cairn-marked way, we climb (N then NE) along a broad shoulder of good rock patched with *carritx*, rock rose and pine, in full view of both the sole and the heel of 'the clog', respectively the **Mola de s'Esclop** and **Es Moletó**. The way veers round to a more easterly direction, initially toward the toe then toward the sole of the clog, passing a pine couchant (Wp.9 37M). The

'Pine Couchant' Wp.9

scrub becomes more invasive here and care must be taken to follow the cairns as we continue climbing, briefly out of sight of the clog.

The full sweep of **S'Esclop** comes back into view beside a large cairn and

'Wp.10' Pine

a mature pine tree with two main trunks (Wp.10 44M). Off to the right, directly in line with the green dip dividing the sole and the heel of the clog, you should be able to pick out the hump of a wall with a ladder stile. After picking our way across a shallow plain, we climb rising rock to reach the ladder stile (Wp.11 50M), a type that is, rather engagingly, called a *botador* in Mallorquin, *bota* being a boot.

Climbing the stile, we enter the **Alquerioles** estate, where the rough walking continues, though the route is easier as patches of reddish dirt pick out something approximating a path weaving through the rocks. We head for the back part of the sole, which we can now see is not a uniform line of rock, as it appeared from below, but a series of folds interleaving with one another. After dropping down to a mini-*coll* (Wp.12 56M), we climb across the rocks (E) on a reasonable path to cross a black water pipe and broken down wall (Wp.13 59M) from where we can see the Alquerioles farmhouse off to our left.

The path appears to be heading directly for the farmhouse, but it soon veers further left (NW), passing 150 metres to the west of the house, where we pass a second pine couchant, this one with a large slab of rock perched on the bole of the trunk (Wp.14 66M). 200 metres later, we cross a second ladder-stile (Wp.15 70M), and all traces of paths, ways, cairns or anything that looks remotely walkable seem to

'Wp.14'

disappear altogether in a dense stand of trees choked with *carritx*. The next 150 metres call for close attention.

The Well at Wp.16

Passing to the left of the first very broad pile of stones immediately after the stile and crossing the second, on which there should be a cairn, we reach the roofless ruin of a tiny cabin, some 75 metres from the stile. On the near side of the cabin, an infinitely faint way winds through the *carritx* onto a retaining wall, which we follow for 10 metres then bear right and wind through more dense *carritx* to reach two relatively clear terraces. 30 metres to our right is an old well (Wp.16 75M) and directly behind it a second, even smaller ruin. Just behind the ruin, a red dot on a retaining wall marks the start of a very obscure way climbing through the *carritx* (NE) to another retaining wall overlooking the pasture behind the **Alquerioles** farm. We climb another 15 metres, at which point (Wp.17

81M) the red-dotted way swings left along a broad, scrub covered ledge between a low crag (on our right) and a 20 metre drop (off to our left), which we follow (N) up to the **Pas d'en Ponsa**, a tiny pass almost blocked by a pine tree (Wp.18 85M), beyond which we see **Estellencs** for the first time.

Approaching Pas d'en Ponsa at Wp.18

That's perhaps the most difficult pathfinding exercise on the stage, but don't relax yet, as we are now entering the wildest part of the walk, traversing the lower slopes of **S'Esclop**. There is no longer any dense vegetation to deal with, but neither are there any paths and it is absolutely essentially to follow the cairn marked routes. Anything that goes anywhere without the benefit of cairns is something that goes somewhere you most emphatically don't want to go!

Immediately after the **Pas d'en Ponsa** pine, we ignore the clear patch of path directly ahead of us (it's the way into all sorts of hellish difficulties) and turn right to climb across the rocks (SE) on a cairn-marked route that brings us onto a rise, within sight once again of the **Mola de s'Esclop** (Wp.19 92M). We continue climbing from cairn to cairn (E), pausing once in a while to enjoy the fabulous views opening out to the west, until we reach rough pasture at the foot of the summit, where we pass between two large sheepfolds (Wp.20 101M).

Bearing left, we follow a rough but slightly clearer way marked with less frequent cairns descending (N) across crumbling terraces toward a solitary pine below a cleft crag, 100 metres short of which a faint path resolves itself amid the scrub. Passing 25 metres below the solitary pine (Wp.21 108M), we head toward a second solitary pine, which we go to the right of (Wp.22 110M), bringing into view **Galatzó**, the triangular mountain that dominates most

Es Castellet & Coll de Font des Quer

views from the southwest.

Immediately in front of us is a long ridge with a distinct hump of rock at its right hand end, known as **Es Castellet**. Behind it and a little to the left, we can pick out a second ridge, the **Serra des Pinotells**. Our descent lies between these two ridges. First though, we must cross the **Coll de Font des Quer**, the obvious *coll* (actually more like a plateau when you reach it) to the right of **Es Castellet**.

Overlooking Es Grau near Wp.24

Aiming for the *coll*, we descend on a narrow path to a Y-junction (Wp.23 112M). Forking left, we continue descending to the left of a long spill of boulders, below which we join a clearer path beside a large protruding rock (Wp.24 116M), part of a classic ascent of **S'Esclop** from the **Es Grau** estate, which is visible below us. Bearing right, we climb to the **Coll de Font des Quer** (Wp.25 119M).

the ruin

Following a faint, flat, grassy path across the plateau behind the *coll*, heading directly toward **Galatzó** (E), we soon see a substantial ruin, 30 metres behind which, we cross a large threshing circle (Wp.26 123M). Ignoring a large cairn off to the right immediately after the threshing circle, we carry straight on (NE), heading

slightly to the right of the **Serra des Pinotells**, below which we can see the corner of a wall. It's worth fixing this direction in mind as the path is frequently obscured by *carritx* and occasionally disappears altogether, but if you aim for the wall, you shouldn't encounter any difficulties.

The threshing circle, with Esclop behind.

Once at the wall, we leave the wayposted path that continues along its near side and climb over the wall (Wp.27 132M), currently at a cairn-marked breach in the topping fence, though I would imagine before long by a signposted stile since this is the way into the **Coma d'en Vidal** estate, bought by the government in 2002

Wp.27

and site of the newly restored refuge. On the far side of the wall, we bear left on a broad trail descending amid a froth of verdant young pine.

The trail soon veers round to the north and broadens to an overgrown dirt track. Doubling back to the left at a junction with two branches that continue to the northeast

(Wp.28 141M), we stay on the main track, descending along the valley to reach the refuge (closed at present, but with an unlocked and recently restored well and porches for shelter if required) (Wp.29 146M).

To carry on to **Estellencs**, we simply follow the main access track out of the refuge. After a long descent, we join another track that climbs from km97 of the MA-10 to the **Boal de ses Serveres**

The Refuge Well

área recreativa (Wp.30 166M). Turning left, we descend toward the road, snaking our way through a succession of tight bends till we come to a long left hand bend surfaced with concrete patterned to appear paved. At the lower end of the concrete, directly in front of a small cistern, we turn right (Wp.31 172M) on a broad, unmarked trail descending to cross the road at km 96.7 (Wp.32 176M).

Crossing the road, we take another broad trail descending in a northwesterly direction (away from **Estellencs**) that soon swings round to the right to join a dirt track, a stretch of the *Carretera Vella* or old road (Wp.33 181M). Turning right, we follow the track till, just below the MA-10, it comes to a Y-junction, where we fork left (Wp.34 188M). The branch track ends 100 metres later, but going through a gateway in a fence above the outlet for a culvert, we walk along the embankment of the MA-10 for a few metres to join another trail that emerges on the road at the **Coll des Pi** (Wp.35 193M).

Bearing left, we follow the road for just over 200 metres before doubling back to the left on a narrow lane (Wp.36 197M) marked with a most singular item, our first GR signpost! The lane snakes its way down into the valley on the near side of **Estellencs** to reach a junction distinguished with our first GR waypost, which we acknowledge by turning right as it suggests (Wp.37 205M).

the first GR Signpost

At a second junction and second waypost, we bear right (Wp.38 214M), arriving in **Estellencs** in front of the Hotel Maristel (Wp.39 219M). The Sa Plana Petit Hotel and the bus-stop for **Banyalbufar** are immediately on the right. Hotel Nord is signposted on the left shortly after we reach the built up area. Stage 3 begins 175 metres on the left at the eastern end of the village .

the first GR Waypost

The Perils of Science

At first glance, you wouldn't have thought that a man like François Arago, the nineteenth century French astronomer, mathematician, physician and politician, who became an academician at the tender age of twenty-three, would have had much time for a wild and inhospitable place like the **Mola d'Esclop** (Stage Two), and yet it was in large measure thanks to this little lump of rock that he established himself as a famous scientist at such a young age.

Employed by the Paris Observatory in the French meridional survey (they couldn't be doing with that English thing running through Greenwich), Arago spent a couple of years in the Spanish mountains establishing various points of latitude and determining the varying force of gravity in each, fetching up in **Mallorca** in 1808 and settling in a small cabin on the summit of **Esclop** with a view to measuring a meridian arc determining the exact length of a metre.

Galatzo from below Esclop

Arago's Eyrie

Unfortunately, though he may have been a dab hand at latitude and longitude, Arago's timing was not otherwise impeccable, because his arrival in Mallorca coincided with the Spanish leg of Napoleon's world tour, an invasion that some people maintain to this day was partly motivated by the Little Emperor's desire to steal the recipes of Spanish cheeses - I'm not making this up! I say his timing was poor, but to be fair Arago was perhaps just being a bit bloody-minded, determined to complete his scientific researches come what may; somewhat more prudently, his colleague, Jean-Baptist Biot, fled to France the moment Napoleon installed his brother Joseph Bonaparte as ruler of Spain. Arago, meanwhile, disguised himself as a peasant, albeit a peasant possessed of a lot of costly scientific equipment.

In the circumstances, the Mallorcans took an understandably dim view of a French official sitting incognito on top of a remote mountain and setting mysterious fires in the dark of the night when any number of nefarious Frenchmen might be out there in their nefarious French fleets nursing their nefarious French intentions, and the hapless scientist was imprisoned in the Bellver fortress in Palma on suspicion of being a nefarious French spy. Thereafter, he engaged in a series of misadventures that would have done a penny-dreadful proud.

Escaping from prison with the connivance of the fort's philomathic commander and absconding in a fishing boat, Arago fled to Algeria where he took passage for France. Unhappily, within sight of Marseille, the ship was captured by a Spanish privateer, and Arago was locked up again, first at Roses and then at Palamos on the Catalan coast. After three months inside, Arago managed to persuade his captors that he really was a scientist and not a spy, whereupon he was released and again set sail for Marseille, only to get caught in a gale and blown back to North Africa by strong northerly winds that deposited him in the obscure port of Béjaïa, where he was jailed yet again, this time by the local potentate. Currying favour by promising to convert to Islam, Arago got himself out of choky for the third time and, with no sea transit available for the next three months, walked the 220 kilometres to Algiers, where he was (yup, you've guessed it, he seems to have had 'issues' when it came to people who possessed big keys and dark cells) duly incarcerated and informed that he'd shortly be shipped off to a penal colony. Released thanks to the intercession of the French consul, he hung about for a further six months before finally embarking for and actually landing in Marseille, where he was promptly banged up in the lazar house for three months' quarantine!

The most remarkable thing about all this though was that, despite all his mishaps, Arago had managed to preserve the log-book detailing his scientific data, an achievement that earned him his place in the French Academy of Sciences and kick-started what proved to be a brilliant career. The roofless remains of his hut on top of **S'Esclop**, which aren't actually visible from the *Ruta de Pedra en Sec*, are nothing very spectacular, but taken as a monument to a man who no amount of dry-stone could keep pinned down, their airy outlook on the arena of his youthful escapades is a more appropriate tribute than having a statue raised to your memory and becoming a public convenience for the benefit of every passing pigeon.

Local pride is a powerful thing and the residents of **Estellencs** and **Banyalbufar** probably won't thank me for lumping the two together, but there is a certain logic to it, one dictated not merely by proximity, but also by a physical and emotional resemblance.

Despite the fact that the Arabic origins of the latter's name suggest it is at sea level, both settlements are perched on what is effectively a narrow ledge between the **Tramuntana** and the Mediterranean, both have tiny ports a short stroll from the main village (closer than usual in Mallorca due to the crowding cliffs preventing a further retreat into the hinterland), and both are rather sleepy little places that appear to be largely overlooked by most visitors, despite having plenty of hotels and hostals - a positively disproportionate number in the case of **Banyalbufar**.

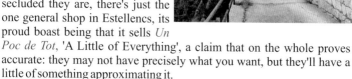

Hostal Baronia Banyalbufar

To give an idea of just how secluded they are, there's just the one general shop in Estellencs, its proud boast being that it sells *Un Poc de Tot*, 'A Little of Everything', a claim that on the whole proves accurate: they may not have precisely what you want, but they'll have a little of something approximating it.

Stroll around the steep streets of either village and you get the distinct impression that very little has changed in the last two hundred years. I'm not saying these places are undiscovered. The chances are that you'll hear as many English and German voices as Mallorcan. But their 'discovery' hasn't exactly been a Eureka-moment of "Let's bus in the tourists and build a big bank to squirrel away all our

money". The 'discovery', if discovery there was, was rather more in the line of: "This is nice. Better keep quiet about this. Wouldn't want it spoiled".

Doubtless space played it's part, there simply isn't the room to develop large scale tourism, but given the leisurely air that prevails, I suspect it never occurred to anybody that these peaceful little enclaves might be the source of large quantities of dosh. Indeed, though I might be doing an injustice to a region that is in truth a hive of economic activity (my apologies if that's the case, but I'm an incurable romantic), spend a little time in either of these villages, particularly in the morning, and you start to wonder whether making money is an issue at all.

Nobody looks particularly wealthy (despite the fact that Richard Branson used to have a house nearby and several of the cliff-top villas are of a magnitude and magnificence that must presuppose a Branson-like fortune), but nobody seems particularly given to getting wealth, either. I certainly didn't see anything that bore a resemblance to 'going to work' and it's a condition to which I'm acutely sensitive, having renounced anything very work-like myself several years ago.

Instead, they wander about, greet the neighbours, possibly purchase a loaf of bread, take the air, stare vaguely out to sea for awhile, greet one another again, sit on the wall for a few moments, perhaps watch the morning bus arrive, then wander about a bit again. It's all really very agreeable. The only sign that there's anything much going on is the flash of welding sparks from the local sculptor's house and a very small door with a sign identifying it as the branch office of the socialist party, which must be hard work on an island that is instinctively conservative. The modernist painter and writer Santiago

'taking the air'

Rusiñol dubbed **Mallorca** *La Illa de la Calma* and it is an injunction the residents of this stretch of the coast seem to have taken to heart.

It's worth, perhaps, paraphrasing here the opening lines of *La Illa de la Calma*, which go something like this: *If you're at your wits end, or think you are, which amounts to the same thing, if you're dazed and confused by the noise of civilization and the haste to get someplace where you find you have nothing to do, if busyness has swamped your brain with facts and science blinded you with gimmickry; then follow me to an island where calm reigns, where the men never hurry and the women never age, and even the sun and the moon move at a more leisurely pace.*

Sounds good to me. Reckon I'm going to wander about a bit. Possibly purchase a loaf of bread. *Un Poc de Tot.* It's enough.

Es Collet

coast after Estellencs

two signs . . .

two stories . . .

Banyalbufar

Banyalbufar

Cami des Correu

Son Bunyola

After the off-path antics involved in negotiating the **Mola de S'Esclop**, Stage Three ought, by rights, to be a lovely relaxing day ambling along well made paths traversing delightful woodland and gazing at the grand spectacle of the rugged northern coast, all the while following a route that has been clearly GR sign and wayposted for several years. In part, that is precisely what it is. There is, however, one significant bugbear and that bugbear, I am afraid to say, is English.

The **Es Rafal** estate between **Estellencs** and **Banyalbufar** was bought some years back by an Englishman who apparently decided a good way of endearing himself to the local population was to institute legal proceedings closing down the ancient bridleway crossing his new property. These have now borne fruit and the path is legally closed. My feelings towards a foreigner (and a compatriot to boot) who buys a large estate including a centuries old right-of-way then contrives to close the thing down are unprintable and very probably libellous. Suffice to say, I was disgruntled enough to include the itinerary in Walk! Mallorca (West) when the route was still sub-judice, since it seemed only fair that English walkers should do their bit to counter problems created by English landowners. Now that the path is legally closed, all I can do is sit in a corner and rant quietly to myself.

The local authorities are contesting the case, so it is always possible that common sense and the public interest will prevail, though I confess, I'm a little pessimistic. Nonetheless, in the wild hope that the path will be re-opened, I am publishing a brief description of the route plus the usual GPS files - simply a reversal of the directions that appeared in the previous publication when we walked it in the opposite direction.

In the meantime, I had planned to trailblaze an alternative route via the **Planícia** estate which is due to be brought into the public domain by government purchase. Unfortunately, when we were researching this book, the sale had not yet been completed. The owners of the estate said 'legal problems' were hampering the transaction, though they were confident the deal would go ahead eventually - albeit not so confident as to open their gates to all and sundry. Other local residents (who all have *'Planícia per à Mallorca'* banners on their balconies) said it was because the owners didn't want to sell the place at the price the government were offering! Either way, the interesting alternatives such a purchase would open up will have to wait till another edition.

Unless the **Es Rafal** path is re-opened (see the websites cited in the Introduction and Appendix E for up-to-date information), I strongly recommend that you skip the first half of Stage Three, for though the start is very pleasant, the long stretch of road walking resulting from the closure of **Es Rafal** has nothing to recommend it.

All is not lost, though. There is a good bus service between **Estellencs** and

Banyalbufar, where we pick up the *Camí des Correu*, the 'Mail Path', a fabulous trail traversing one of the loveliest oak woods on the island. It's a popular route, but every time I do it I'm taken aback by just how lovely it is and can understand all too well why so many people, plenty of them clearly not habitual walkers, regard this as one of the great Sunday outings. Once you've done it, I'm sure you'll agree. Frankly, if this is the Mail Path, I'm going to chuck it all in and become a postman. Blow the writing! I want to deliver the letters. The *Camí des Correu* has been beautifully restored and is immaculately wayposted, so once you're on it, stow the book and just enjoy. It's a delight.

3A. Estellencs to Banyalbufar

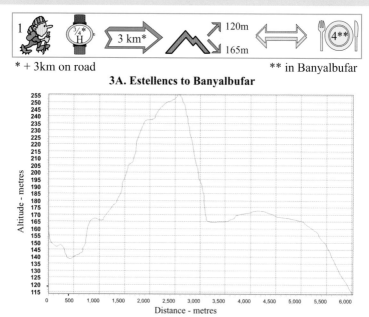

* + 3km on road
** in Banyalbufar

3A. Estellencs to Banyalbufar

From the entrance to the car-park in front of the *lavadero* at the eastern end of **Estellencs** (Wp.1 0M), we follow the MA-10 past the 'Pizzeria Siardini' for 150-metres, then fork left on a concrete track (Wp.2), where there are GR signposts and a metal sign advising us that the path is closed after 4.5 kilometres.

When the track bottoms out after 75 metres, we fork left on a narrow path (Wp.3) that soon reveals itself to be the remains of an old cobbled trail. The trail, which is clearly wayposted throughout, crosses another concrete track and a paved way descending to the left, then skirts the **Es Collet** driveway before rejoining the MA-10 (Wp.4 12M).

Turning left, we follow the road for 700 metres then fork right on a roughly concreted track (Wp.5 19M) climbing to the north of **Son**

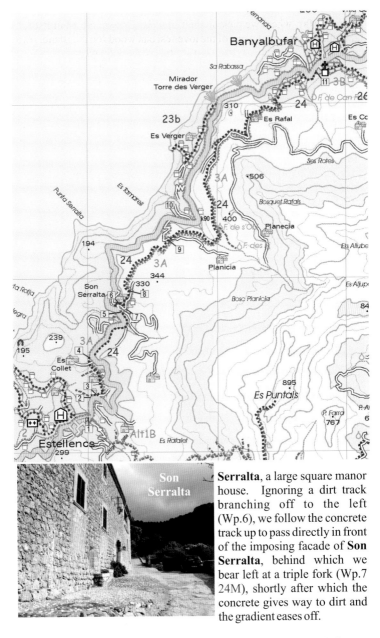

Serralta, a large square manor house. Ignoring a dirt track branching off to the left (Wp.6), we follow the concrete track up to pass directly in front of the imposing facade of **Son Serralta**, behind which we bear left at a triple fork (Wp.7 24M), shortly after which the concrete gives way to dirt and the gradient eases off.

When the track goes through a gate 75 metres later, we fork left on a narrow path running along an equally narrow terrace (Wp.8 26M). The path traverses attractive mixed woodland with lovely sea views glimpsed through the interlacing branches, then climbs to cross a small *coll* where there's a GR signpost. Hereafter, Holm Oak predominate, giving us a taste of the superb woodland that characterized the old route. Alas, all too soon, we emerge on the **Planícia** access lane (Wp.9 38M), which is not actually the point where the GR has been closed, but is the only place where there's an easy way down to the road.

If the closure signs are still in place, all we can do now (apart from trespassing, which I wouldn't recommend, though it's sorely tempting) is turn left, descend to the road (Wp.10 44M), and stick our thumbs out to cover the three kilometres to **Banyalbufar** city limits (Wp.11).

In the event that the **Es Rafal** path is re-opened, here is a brief description of the remaining route after Wp.9. The path was walked in the opposite direction in 2005, so the GPS files are old and the description is simply a reversal of what I noted then. This information is contained in separate GPS files titled 'Stage 3 Lost Path via Es Rafal'. The waypoints carry an 'LP' prefix for the obvious, lamentable reason. The timings here are approximate. Needless to say, if the path has reopened and follows a different route to the one described, follow the wayposts.

Following the wayposted path on the far side of the **Planícia** access lane (Wp.LP01 0M), we wind through lovely pine and oak woods to reach a junction just short of the **Torrent de Can Cerdá** (Wp.LP02). Crossing the torrent, we climb to a second junction near the **Font de s'Obi**, at which point we turn left (Wp.LP03 15M). 400 metres later, we go through a gate into the **Es Rafal** estate (Wp.LP04 25M).

cabin near
Font de s'Obi

After following a track along a terrace, we ignore a minor branch descending to the left (Wp.LP05) and climb to another junction where we turn right (Wp.LP06 33M), climbing along a broad, curving terrace. Carrying straight on at an inverted Y-junction (Wp.LP07 35M) then bearing right as the track approaches the **Es Rafal** farmhouse (Wp.LP08), we go between the house and a threshing circle, 75 metres after which we leave the Es Rafal estate via green gates (Wp.LP09 45M).

Thereafter, we descend along a stepped path that soon broadens to become a dirt track (Wp.LP10 50M). The track brings us down to a narrow lane (Wp.LP11) leading to the MA-10 and the Son Tomas restaurant at the western limit of **Banyalbufar** (Wp.LP12 65M).

If you're starting your walk from **Banyalbufar** to avoid the accommodation and pathfinding hassles of Stages One and Two, what you do rather depends on how much time you have on the day of arrival, how much time you have overall, and how much you're prepared to splash out on accommodation. It's worth noting though that Stage 3B (like Stage 1A and the two alternative starts) is ideal for a good short walk on the first day. If you're arriving too late to set off directly, you might consider combining Stages 3B and 4A, preserving the **Teix** traverse for a leisurely but indulgent second day, or pushing on from **Deià** to include Stage Five in your second day's walking.

* in the villages

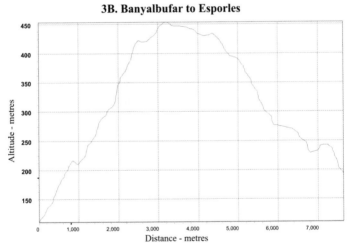

3B. Banyalbufar to Esporles

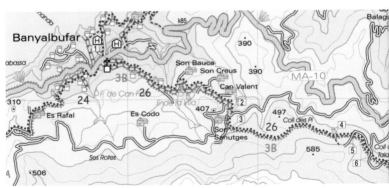

We set off from 'Plaza de la Vila', the elevated square in front of the *ayuntamiento* directly above **Banyalbufar**'s central bus-stops, on the narrow street climbing to the left of the town hall, 'Carrer Jeroni Alberti' (Wp.1 0M). Jeroni Alberti becomes 'Carrer de Font de la Vila' and we pass a GR sign on the wall announcing 'Esporles Camí des Correu 2h30', after which we leave the housing behind and the street becomes an attractive lane climbing steeply into the terraced countryside surrounding the village.

We follow this lane <u>all</u> the way to the <u>very</u> end (you'll soon understand the emphasis), climbing steadily to steeply, ignoring all branch tracks and paths. After what seems like forever (in fact, only one-and-a-half kilometres), we pass the entrance to 'Can Valent', and the tarmac gives way to concrete for the last couple of hundred metres, at the end of which we come to a crossroads with a dirt track on the edge of the **Son Sanutges** estate (Wp.2 29M).

Carrying straight on, we cross the dirt track and follow a signposted trail, concreted for the first few metres and broad enough to look like a track, but soon dwindling to the intermittently cobbled trail of the *Camí des Correu*. The trail runs alongside the **Son Sanutges** fence, swinging left at a junction with the dirt track on the far side of the fence (Wp.3 33M), after which we enter the Holm Oak wood. The *camí* continues to climb steadily for the first couple of hundred metres, then levels off as we cross two broken walls.

approaching Coll des Pi

Son Bunyola

At this point, you will begin to appreciate why it was worth slogging up that lane, and why quite so many people regard this path as a good reason to skip church, visiting the relatives, having a nap in front of the TV, stuffing themselves silly with *paella*, or whatever other Sunday inactivity you care to name. After a stroll so sweet it could provoke diabetes, we come to a long section of paved trail that climbs gently into woodland where the pine predominate, though there are also plenty of strawberry trees, and we cross, probably without noticing, the appropriately named **Coll des Pi**.

After the imperceptible *coll*, the *camí* levels off again and views open out

Sa Foradada

over the coast down toward **Port des Canonge** and the big block-like manor house of **Son Bunyola**, formerly Richard Branson's little place in the country and more recently the object of a money laundering scandal involving a man named Hoare - honestly, I read it in the papers.

We can also see the **Teix** massif, which we will cross in Stage 4B Wps.6-10. **Puig Veia** (also spelled Vella) is the summit on the left directly in line with **Sa Foradada**, the distinct spit of rock poking out into the sea; behind **Puig Veia** we can pick out a patch of the **Cingles de Son Rullan** and the little hump of **Puig Caragoli** and, further to the

cliffs north of Puig Veia

right, in the middle of the intervening valley, the high cliffs of the **Mola de son Ferrandell**, which we pass behind in Stage 4A (Wps. 8-18).

The woodland soon closes in again, cutting off the views except for brief glimpses through the trees. Passing an ancient, obscure trail doubling back to the right (Wp.4 54M) and, 50 metres later, a particularly fine limekiln, we continue with our cultivation of an ever more acute case of diabetes. Carrying straight on at a crossroads with a dirt track (Wp.5 57M) and a broad trail (Wp.6 62M), we cross another imperceptible *coll* (**Coll de sa Talaieta**) at a sign indicating 'Esporles 40m'.

We now descend through a series of zigzags to a long straight stretch leading to a patch of paving, at the end of which we carry straight on (Wp.7 71M) alongside a wall for a final descent through the woods. After passing another limekiln and two very faint paths forking off to the right

within 50 metres of one another (so faint you may not even notice them) (Wp.8 77M), we go through a gate, beyond which the woodland gives way to abandoned terraces.

A couple of hundred metres after a second gate, the trail emerges on the MA-1120 (Wp.9 89M). Crossing the road, we follow a newly made path shadowing the road past the turning to 'Puigpunyent' and 'La Granja', a large country house that is now a popular tourist attraction. 50 metres after a bend in the old road, we recross the MA-1120 (Wp.10 100M) to join a dirt track climbing to a Y-junction in front of a gate into a field (Wp.11 105M).

Forking right, we follow a bridleway that brings us into **Esporles** at the bend of a lane behind the church (Wp.12 111M). Carrying straight on, we descend to the church, where we bear left, passing in front of the Hotel l'Estada to join the main road in front of the **Esporles** *ayuntamiento* (Wp.13 114M). 25 metres on our right is the highly recommended Ca'n Oliveret bakery. The GR for **Valldemossa** continues 15 metres to the left.

Whereas **Estellencs** and **Banyalbufar**, from an outsider's perspective, at least, can be comfortably lumped together, **Esporles** and **Valldemossa** share little apart from topography and (not such a small thing when it comes down to it) two of the best bakers on the island. Both are located toward the top of valleys feeding into the southern plain, both are separated from their respective ports, **Port d'es Canonge** and **Port de Valldemossa**, by towering cliffs and tightly twisting roads, both are surrounded by olive groves and Holm Oak forests, and both are very pretty; but there the similarities end.

Given the popularity of the *Camí des Correu* climbing from **Banyalbufar**, you see plenty of hiking parties in **Esporles**, but it's not really a town that's on the tourist trail, which can seem a little puzzling at first because it's a lovely place, and only lacks a celebrity or a single outstanding monument to put it on the map and draw the tour buses in. Needless to say, this is a want that can only be commended. That said, the town's charms aren't exactly secret and some locals complain that it grows more crowded by the year as expats and commuters decide that, in the first instance, this is a bit of the 'real' **Mallorca** they want to be a part of, and, in the second, that living in a peaceful rural community twenty minutes from the capital is a lot nicer than being crowded into a noisy flat on the outskirts of **Palma**.

Ermita de Maristel, Esporles

Sunday morning in Esporles

If you have the time, it's well worth whiling away a Sunday morning sat in front of one of the bars on the high street, nursing a *café con leche* and a copy of that most admirable of newspapers, El Pais, while simply watching the world go by. If that's not an option, then at the very least you should stop off at the excellent Ca'n Oliveret bakery. Their *pan aleman* is sufficiently substantial to be used as ballast in a small boat, anyone fond of a pork pie simply has to try their *empanada de carne con guisantes*, and the *coca's* not half bad either.

Also highly commended is the *coca* at the Es Cos bakery next to the Arte de Toledo gift shop in the centre of **Valldemossa**, which is distant enough for you to have worked up an appetite en route from Ca'n Oliveret. At first glance, **Valldemossa** is everything that **Esporles** is not, a place swamped by its own fame, crawling with coaches, swarming with day-trippers, every shop stacked with the sort of upmarket tack that looks very nice on the shelves but when you get it home you wonder, "What did I want with this?" And yet you can understand why it has become so popular and, if you spend a little time there, appreciate that the people have been quite artful in exploiting without denaturing the picturesque qualities that have engendered the town's popularity.

La Cartoixa

Among the first outsiders to appreciate Valldemossa's beauty were the Carthusian monks (funny, isn't it, how such otherworldly entities as monastic orders never settle in ugly places) who rolled up in the fifteenth century and thought it was such a fine spot they persuaded King Don Martí (described by Rusiñol as "a man of such piety, nobody has a word to say about him, either good or bad"!) to give them the remains of the old royal palace. When the order was disentailed some three hundred years later, its Spanish properties were variously sacked by embittered tenants or sold into private hands. Being a practical people, the Valldemossans opted for the latter solution, kick-starting their enterprise with an impressive publicity coup by renting out a couple of cells to Europe's most fêted artistic couple, George Sand and Frederic Chopin. The famous visitors have continued ever since and the chances are that nowadays you'll see Michael Douglas' face plastered across municipal billboards if not the man himself, for he currently owns one of the Archduke Ludwig Salvador's houses on the coast.

hidden corners of Valledemossa

Catch **Valldemossa** at the wrong time and the first instinct for someone who likes wild places and getting off the beaten track is a sort of urgent Beam-me-up-Scotty moment, but it's worth resisting that instinct because it really is a very pretty place and maintains an authentic life of its own, perhaps best seen by watching the early morning comings and goings in the Bar Merienda where the locals foregather. If you're staying overnight, indulge yourself in a leisurely stroll round the town (evening or morning, either way when the coach-parties aren't cluttering up the place) just breathing in the atmosphere that has beguiled so many literary celebrities, taking in the odd architectural details and tiny hidden corners that are tucked away in virtually every street, and perhaps comparing the varying scenes depicted in the numerous Santa Catalina Thomas plaques.

hidden corners of Valledemossa

The Valldemossans don't look uncommonly devout, but almost without exception, every house in the town has a ceramic tile cemented to the wall illustrating the infancy of local girl Santa Catalina Thomas, a sixteenth century nun so thoroughly self-effacing I haven't actually been able to work out quite why she was beatified, though I believe she was given to visions and made a powerful impression on her coevals by her flair for epiphanies, which appear to have been at once copious and, one would have thought, a little wearing.

SANTA CATALINA THOMAS PREGAU PER NOSALTRES

Santa Catalina Thomas

For more information, see:

- www.ajesporles.net (in Catalan and Spanish) or check out the Esporles page on the www.mca-hotels.com holiday-guides Mallorca page, which is also quite good for the other towns crossed by the GR

- www.lagranja.net explaining what can be seen and done at the eponymous tourist attraction

- www.valldemossa.com, a thorough general site, apparently not available in English, but relatively easy to navigate even with rudimentary Spanish

- www.info-mallorca.co.uk/valldemossa for a good selection of photos

Sa Basseta woods

the cliff path

Son Cabaspre valley

Pla de l'Aljub cisterns

fairytale woods above Valledemossa

Archduke's path (1)

bucolic scene above Esporles

Archduke's path (2)

Though not one of the GR's most spectacular sections, the first leg of Stage Four, which takes us from **Esporles** to **Valldemossa**, earns its stripes through a deft combination of domesticity and obscurity, featuring an initial climb (mostly on tarmac) through charming, peaceful countryside followed by traverses of a plateau and a ridge that, until now, have rarely been visited by outsiders and on which even Mallorcan ramblers are scarce.

The two traverses are the highlights, particularly the wooded plateau of **Pla de l'Aljub** with its immaculately preserved remains of the rural industries that persisted up here within living memory, above all a fine charcoal burners' bread oven and the twinned cistern/shelter at the heart of the plateau.

For those of you bivouacking out, it's worth noting that the shelter is, at the time of writing, spotless, though you probably wouldn't want to get too intimate with the cistern water. There is also at least one other shelter that could be used if the weather turned nasty. The first stretch of the ascent is well sign and wayposted, but thereafter there are some modest pathfinding problems that oblige us to consult the book en route.

By contrast with the relatively muted charms of the approach to **Valldemossa**, the ongoing route to **Deià** is a clamorous fanfare of blaring horns and boisterous drum rolls, not literally but metaphorically, featuring as it does two trails that are so extraordinary they would justify the cost of flying to the island on their own. The first of these is the celebrated *Camí de s'Arxiduc*.

There was a touch of the Capability Browns about the Archduke Ludwig Salvator in that on occasion he would look at the natural world he loved and declare it 'capable of improvement'. It's a conceit with which modern aficionados of the great outdoors may have some difficulty, but in the case of the bridleway he laid across the **Teix** massive it would be captious to pretend he didn't have a point.

If the word 'bridleway' puts you in mind of a muddy farm track reduced by livestock and agricultural machinery to something resembling a very long midden, think again. This is a bridleway conceived on a scale only a nineteenth century romantic could have dreamed up, a beautifully tailored trail winding along the dizzying cliffs overlooking **Valldemossa** and **Deià**. 'Dizzying' is a term that might alarm certain readers and it's true that some walkers do consider this route vertiginous. Personally, all I can say is that I suffer from vertigo and I find the broad, well-laid Archduke's Path a bit of toe-tingler, but certainly no toe-curler. In any case, if you really don't like the look of the drop, it's always possible to stay back from the edge, as the interior side of the path is rough but gently sloping ground.

Not content with incorporating what may well be the best bridleway in the world, this stretch of the *Ruta de Pedra en Sec* also includes what is probably the most spectacular path on the island, the old charcoal burners' and drovers' trail snaking its way down the **Cingles de Son Rullan** - yup, that's right, *cingles*, 'cliffs'. Seen from below, this route is clearly impossible; seen from the top, it looks highly improbable; but when you're on it, it's a lot easier than it ought to be given that it basically just drops off the edge of the mountain. There is a slight risk of vertigo, but for the most part the way is broad (10-20 metres) and we are shielded from the drops by the Holm Oak that cling to the long sloping shelves by which we make our descent.

Given that this is probably going to be one of your most memorable days walking on the island, I strongly recommend splitting this stage into two. It's perfectly feasible to do it all in one go, but you really don't want to spoil the experience of these two great paths by knocking them off at the end of the day when you're tired. This is an experience to be savoured. Take your time and enjoy!

Part B. between **Valldemossa** and **Deià** is not recommended when visibility is poor or in high winds. Despite its popularity, the path has yet to be signposted, but pathfinding is not a problem and the route is clearly waymarked with cairns.

4A Esporles to Valldemossa

* in towns

4A. Esporles to Valldemossa

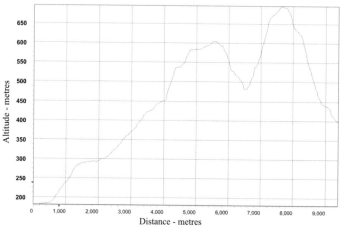

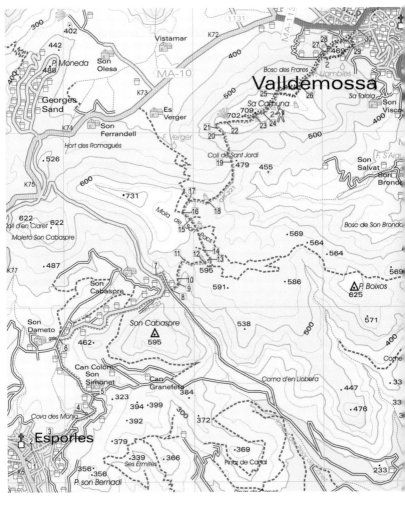

Immediately to the left of **Esporles** *ayuntamiento*, we take 'Carrer Nou de Sant Pere' (Wp.1 0M), crossing a bridge over **Torrent de Sant Pere** and 'Carrer Major' after 150 metres to reach the 'Placeta des Pla' where we bear right (Wp.2). Crossing a second bridge after another 150 metres, we turn

anonymous cottage

left (Wp.3 5M) on a narrow lane climbing alongside the **Son Cabaspre** torrent.

After 500 metres, the lane swings sharp left and we carry straight on along a dirt track (Wp.4 11M), climbing steadily behind a small house to join another lane on which we turn left (Wp.5 15M). Ignoring a

Son Dameto

branch doubling back to the right 100 metres later, we follow this lane all the way to the gates of the **Son Cabaspre** *urbanización*, enjoying fine views off to the west of the **Planìcia** and **Fita del Ram** massifs, the latter spotted with the white walls of the **Ermita de Maristella** chapel and, lower down, a

rather groovy (looks like he's jiving from close up) statue of Jesus. We're also distracted from the tarmac by lovely countryside, views of the cliffs below the **Mola de Son Ferrandell**, and some appealing examples of vernacular architecture, ranging from the very humble and anonymous to the rather grand **Son Dameto**.

waypoint 7

CAMI DE SA COMA LLOBERA

50 metres after going through the **Son Cabaspre** *urbanización* gateway, we turn right on the 'Camí des Bosc' (Wp.6 27M), a broad roughly surfaced lane skirting the southern perimeter of the *urbanización*. At length (possibly a little too much length for some tastes, we have after all done over three kilometres on asphalt), the lane swings round to the left (N), and we turn right on the 'Camí de sa Llobera' (Wp.7 48M), a track climbing to reach the **Coll de sa Basseta** 200 metres later (Wp.8 52M), where there's a small concrete pond and what, for the present, proves to be our last bit of wayposting for a while, a sign indicating 'Esporles 1h' back in the direction we've just come. This is where the mild pathfinding problems begin, though there are a number of cairns and a few small yellow arrow heads made of chipboard with a reflector band stuck onto the base.

a sign that has seen better days

Turning left at the *coll*, we immediately fork right on a faint trail marked with a cairn, an ancient red dot, and a plywood sign that looks like it has seen better days and won't see a lot more. If the sign is no longer there and nothing new has replaced it, this path starts 10 metres above the *coll* at the first bend of the roughly concreted track that ends at a small house 100 metres later. Once you're on it, the path is perfectly clear to begin with, climbing steeply amid scattered Holm Oak, pine and strawberry trees, alongside a long sloping outcrop of rock peppered with pine trees growing out of the most improbable crevices. At the top of the outcrop of rock, we bear left above double *sitjes*, where there maybe a hunter's hide (for netting small birds rather than blasting away at what the islanders like to call 'Big Game' i.e. goats) (Wp.9 57M), and climb along an obscure, cairn-marked way (N) to cross

'improbable growth'

waypoint 9

a wall 50 metres later beside a blocked gateway (Wp.10).

The path becomes clearer beyond the wall, but the cairns still help us pick out its slightly devious course as it weaves between the rocks (NNE), bringing us back into lovely dense woodland, comparable to that on the *Camí des Correu* only in this instance a little wilder. Passing directly below a *sitja* (Wp.11 64M), we veer round to a more easterly direction, and views open out across the southern plain. After a gentle climb, the path levels out, passing the ruins of a small charcoal burning settlement, immediately after which we join a broad, stony track (Wp.12 69M).

Bearing left then turning left at a junction 75 metres later (Wp.13), we stroll across the **Pla de l'Aljub** (N), ignoring a faint branch off to the left after 125 metres (Wp.14). Likewise, 125 metres after a second charcoal burners' settlement, we ignore a faint branch off to the right (Wp.15), from where we can already glimpse through the trees the walls of the *aljub* or cistern that gives the plain its name. The shelter mentioned in the introduction, which appears to be a converted *aljub*, stands beside the main cistern.

At the Y-junction immediately to the east of the two constructions (Wp.16 80M), we fork right then right again

bread oven

aljub

30 metres later toward the northeastern edge of the plateau and the second slightly tricky bit of pathfinding. At the next Y-junction beside a mossy *sitja*, the ruins of a cabin and, behind it amid the trees, a bread oven, we fork right, passing to the south of the *sitja*/cabin on the fainter of the two branches, which also happens to be the one NOT marked with a cairn (Wp.17 82M).

75 metres later, we bear right alongside a wall (though it's worth noting that there's an excellent natural *mirador* 25 metres to the left) to follow a tiny path marked with cairns and ancient red waymarks. The path becomes clearer as the trees become denser, though it's still comforting to see the occasional cairn and waymark - stray off path up here and you could wander about in circles for decades! After descending (SE) to pass another double *sitja*, the path veers left and drops down to cross a small wall blocking a rocky declivity (Wp.18 89M).

Following a generally clear but consistently rough path, we descend steeply through a tangle of woodland down to a new fence, where the path swings left, bringing into view the daunting southern face of the **Sa Comuna** ridge before resuming its steep descent between the new fence and the fence-topped wall of the **Son Ferrandell** estate. The path levels out for a while, hemmed in by wall and fence, then descends again before bottoming out at a GR waypost (somewhat redundant given the lack of wayposting on the *pla* where it would be really useful) and gate on the **Coll de Sant Jordi** (Wp.19 101M) - cue sharp intake of breath as we contemplate the looming rocks of **Sa Comuna**, which we now have to climb; judging by the scattering of fruit peel in various stages of decay, most people stop here to recuperate before the ensuing climb.

Going through the gate and turning right, we begin our second ascent, still hemmed in by fencing, which is presumably designed to prevent trespass but also proves a convenient way of not getting lost. We climb steadily then steeply along a broad trail following the fence on our left, at the end of which (Wp.20 108M), a narrower path zigzags up through the rock on traverses clearly demarcated by retaining walls. Shortly after passing a small overhang where goats and possibly other pedestrians shelter from time to time (Wp.21 115M), views briefly open out toward the coast, but we have little time to appreciate them, because the path promptly veers back toward the southern side of the ridge for the final steep climb.

As the gradient eases off then finally levels out altogether, we pass another superb little *mirador* (Wp.22 123M) from where we can see new housing to the north of **Valldemossa** and the cliffs looming over **Son Moragues** (the large square house directly behind the petrol station and line of plane trees), the first of the Archduke's many homes on Mallorca, purchased when he got stuck in a rainstorm and decided the only sane response was to buy a house. We now follow a rough but unmistakable way just below the ridge favouring its southern flank, climbing slightly from time to time until we reach the first of two low cabins with corrugated roofs (Wp.23 129M) - not hugely salubrious, but not so disgusting that you couldn't take shelter there in an emergency.

Immediately after the second cabin, we cross a wall and carry straight on along a more obscure trail. Descending slightly to the right 75 metres after the wall (Wp.24 133M), we recover a clear path that crosses a *sitja* 100 metres later, beyond which we begin our descent to **Valldemossa**. Winding steeply down the northern flank of the ridge, we pass an open, compartmentalized cistern (Wp.25 138M) and go through a gateway to reach a second covered cistern where a GR signpost indicates, somewhat superfluously, that we take the obvious path down to the left (Wp.26 143M).

After dropping down through a series of very tight bends, the gradient gradually eases off as we approach the first house on the periphery of **Valldemossa**. Directly behind the house, we pass a small spring, the **Font de na Llambies**, and go through a gateway to reach a T-junction 20 metres later with another, narrower path (Wp.27 158M). Turning left then bearing left at the bottom of a stairway less than 50 metres later (Wp.28), we contour round the small rise of the **Moli de sa Beata** to arrive in **Valldemossa** on a concrete lane (Wp.29 163M) behind the **Finca Son Mossenya**, home to the Friends of Jorge Luis Borges association, located here in honour of the great fabulist's brief stay in the town when he was a teenager. Bearing left then left again 75 metres later, we reach the main road where the MA-1110 becomes the MA-1130 (Wp.30). The Tourist Information Office, the first actually on the route of the GR, is 100 metres to the right on the main road. The Es Cos bakery is also on the right, on the narrower road leading into the town centre. For Stage 4B, we cross the road and carry straight on.

* in Valledemossa & Deià

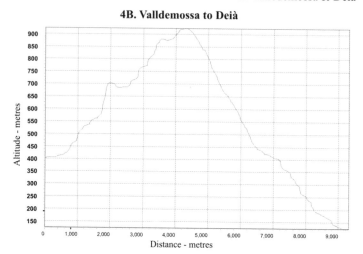

4B. Valldemossa to Deià

From the bus-stop at the northern end of **Valldemossa**, the point at which the MA-10 becomes the MA-1130 (Wp.1 0M), we cross the 'Plaça Camp de Vànol' and carry straight on along the road behind the taxi stand. 75 metres later, we take the second turning on the right (Wp.2) to pass the sports field, beyond which we continue on 'Carrer de Joan Fuster'. We then fork left into 'Carrer de Oliveres' (Wp.3), at the end of which a broad walking trail begins beside the gates of the 'Son Gual Petit' *finca* (Wp.4 8M).

The trail shadows the **Son Gual** driveway, then swings left, climbing to cross a stile (Wp.5 13M), where we ignore branches off to left and right. Thereafter, we climb steadily along a beautifully graded trail winding through sun-dappled woodland. There are a number of shortcuts across bends toward the top, but they serve no great purpose, apart perhaps from encouraging erosion, so we stick with the main route until it goes through a gateway into a flat, wooded area, the **Pla des Pouet**, at the heart of which, 200 metres from the gateway, there's a junction of paths beside a covered well (Wp.6 34M).

The route directly ahead leads to the **Mirador de Ses Puntes**

Pla des Pouet

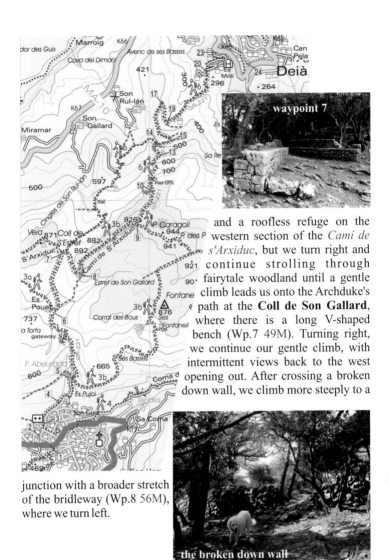

waypoint 7

and a roofless refuge on the western section of the *Camí de s'Arxiduc*, but we turn right and continue strolling through fairytale woodland until a gentle climb leads us onto the Archduke's path at the **Coll de Son Gallard**, where there is a long V-shaped bench (Wp.7 49M). Turning right, we continue our gentle climb, with intermittent views back to the west opening out. After crossing a broken down wall, we climb more steeply to a

junction with a broader stretch of the bridleway (Wp.8 56M), where we turn left.

the broken down wall

Brace yourselves, 200 metres later, we emerge on a superb natural *mirador* overlooking, off to the left, the roofless refuge on **Puig Veia**, and off to the right, the **Cingles de Son Rullan** - that's right, the ones we descend! Don't worry, though, the descent is not via the near cliffs, which are sheer, but the more distant drop clad in woodland. Continuing on the most spectacular part of the bridleway (toes-tingling, no

Puig Veia

doubt), **Teix** comes into view, and a fine perspective opens out onto the pierced rock of **Sa Foradada** on the coast.

After contouring along the edge of the cliffs, we climb across what appears to be a discrete summit, but is in fact the western edge of a plateau preceding the diminutive but distinctively conical peak of **Puig des Caragolí**. At this stage, **Puig Major**, Mallorca's highest mountain, comes into view, and we can make out

the Archduke's Path

Sa Foradada

new white housing climbing the eastern flank of **Port de Sóller**. Ten metres after passing a large pile of stones and a couple of hundred metres short of **Puig des Caragolí**, we turn left between two large cairns (Wp.9 78M), leaving the Archduke's Path and embarking on the second bit of the day's adventure.

From this perspective, it looks to all intents and purposes as if we're just going to walk off the edge of a cliff, which we are in a way, though not in a manner necessarily detrimental to health. Following a clear, stony path waymarked with cairns and another large pile of stones, we descend gently (NE), passing to the right of the main clump of Holm Oak,

waypoint 9

the Cingles Path

where a flurry of cairns marks the head of the *cingles* path (Wp.10 85M). A word to the wise: GPS reception can be poor below these cliffs, but for the next 40 minutes, GPS is strictly for the birds given that anybody trying to maintain a straight line will have to fly.

After a first long sloping shelf

descending steeply amid Holm Oak in an easterly direction, the path veers round to the west on a slightly exposed section then zigzags down to what appears to be another sheer drop, but is in fact another long, easterly traverse, once again shielded by Holm Oak. Immediately after skirting a large rock sticking up in the middle of the path (Wp.11 103M), we pass a gatepost built into the cliff, presumably the remains of a counting gate when descending shepherds checked they still had their entire flock, and fine views open out over the **Son Rullan** farmhouse. 150 metres later, we must take care to double back to the right along the cairn-marked path when a minor branch carries straight on (Wp.12). The woods become denser and deeper as we continue our descent, but we still have to pause to appreciate their beauty, as the rough path means we must watch every step of the way.

Bread Oven at waypoint 14

Trough at waypoint 14

After countless zigzags (possibly somebody's counted them, but it's not the sort of pastime that gets my pulse racing), we pass a *sitja* and the remains of a charcoal burner's cabin (Wp.13 115M). Still winding back and forth like an epileptic snake, the path crosses a second *sitja*, then joins a broader path at a 3rd *sitja* beside a bread oven (Wp.14 120M). Bearing right and crossing the *sitja*, we pass a trough carved into a massive boulder and an interesting combination of a *sitja* and limekiln side by side. Sticking with the cairn-marked route, we ignore two branches off to the right (Wps.15 & 16 127M), after which the woodland thins and pine predominate, and we

Sitja & Limekiln

emerge on a long terrace within sight of **Deià**.

Reaching a gateway in a wall with two very ramshackle rusting gates hanging from their hinges like a couple of sagging drunks (Wp.17 133M), we double back to the right on a narrow initially cobbled path. Look out for the cairns here as this path is increasingly invaded by *carritx* and could disappear altogether if it's not cleared. We zigzag down across terraces, forking left on another cobbled stretch 75 metres before a cabin (visible from the first terrace after Wp.16) (Wp.18 137M), passing a small spring and trough, immediately after which we again fork left (Wp.19).

We now descend on an intermittently cobbled path along the delightful little valley (once cultivated but now abandoned to the *carritx*) that divides the dilapidated stronghold of **Castell des Moro** from the **Can Borràs** farmhouse. The path eventually joins a dirt track in front of **Can Borràs** (Wp.20 159M).

Castell des Moro

Bearing right, we follow this track and the lane it leads into all the way down to the **Hotel Es Molí** car-park, ignoring all branches en route. Directly in front of the hotel, we take the 'Camí de Ca'n Quet' stairway (Wp.21 168M). Emerging on the road (Wp.22), we turn left then right 50 metres later (Wp.23 172M) on a lane that leads to the **Can Boi** refuge at the head of valley below the village (Wp.24 177M).

Go for a walk in the woods pretty much anywhere in the Catalan speaking lands and sooner or later you will stumble upon a manmade glade at the heart of which you will find a flat moss frosted circle of dense, dark soil ringed with a line of stones. This is a pit-stead or charcoal burning hearth, known in Catalan as a *sitja,* the plural of which, *sitjes*, lends its name to the popular resort south of Barcelona.

Until the last century, charcoal was the principal cooking fuel in Mallorca, and much of the countryside is nowadays accessed by the old charcoal-burners' paths linking the low lying villages with the remote *sitjes* in the mountains, where the charcoal burners and their families camped throughout the spring and summer. For modern walkers, this network of paths is an absolute boon, moreover, the *sitjes* themselves and the family's beehive bread ovens provide useful staging posts for directions.

As is so often the case though, what we exploit as a source of pleasure has its origins in a tough, unrewarding life. Charcoal burners were notoriously poor, living in thatched dry stone huts furnished only with a bed made of a heap of stones with a pile of straw for a mattress, and earning barely enough to buy the necessities, yet great skill was required for this delicate and dangerous task. To get an idea of what it involved, just imagine how you would feel if, at the height of summer, your job involved stoking a dirty great fire and clambering all over it to ensure it continued smoldering for ten days, keeping it at just the right temperature to avoid the wood being consumed by flames, and, of course, making sure you didn't burn half the mountain down - and that with only a shovelful of soil to tame the inferno! Worse, the temporary 'ovens' of gravel and clay coating the raw wood were never very stable at the best of times and, as the wood was reduced, they sometimes collapsed. And if you happened to be on top at the time feeding the core fire through the central chimney . . . Well, you get the picture. So when you're barreling along having a whale of a time on a lovely woodland trail, spare a thought for the people who made it.

The other even poorer rural industry that lead to the making of these paths was lime-firing to extract mortar and a wash for whitening houses. The lime kilns or *hornos de calç,* take the form of stone-lined pits (very occasionally still capped with a conical cupola), fine examples of which can be seen on the *Camí des Correu* (Stage Three). In another hugely

unenviable job, limestone was manually crushed then interleaved with wood and fired to a temperature in the order of 900° to produce the quicklime that was scraped out of the oven after the conflagration had cooled down.

Snow gathering for the purposes of preparing medicines and refrigerating food and drink during the summer had less impact on the walking landscape, but was no less important in terms of the island's economy, and was still in operation as late as the 1920s. Trampled into ice and packed between protective layers of *carritx*, the snow was stored in deep pits known as

casas de nieve or snow-houses and then transported down to the plain piecemeal on mules during the summer nights. One of the island's most spectacular and best preserved concentrations of *casas de nieve* is to be found on Stage Seven of the GR221.

In 1867, the Austrian Archduke Ludwig Salvator visited **Mallorca** and liked it so much he stayed, establishing a tradition that has continued unabated to the present day. Ludwig, however, was more ambitious than modern migrants. His season in the sun was conceived on a large scale and, rather than settling for a modest villa by the sea, he instigated a series of grandiose restoration and construction projects, notably of several buildings in the vicinity of **Valldemossa**, including **Son Moragues**, **Son Marroig**, and **S'Estaca**, the current retreat of Michael Douglas.

Nor was Ludwig a man to take his rustic pleasures lightly. Instead of toiling along charcoal burners' paths, he set about improving the **Teix Massif**, laying a bridleway complete with refuges and *miradors*, a rich man's folly for which generations of walkers have been grateful. So enamoured was Ludwig of the landscape that he couldn't bear to cut down the trees on his estates and would instead buy firewood from his neighbours, an eccentricity that was latched upon by wily locals, who knew that if they wanted to sell a patch of land, they only had to let it be known that they were going to clearcut their woods to have the Archduke whipping out his purse.

Had he not come to **Mallorca**, Ludwig, a lowly member of the Habsburg-Lorraine imperial dynasty, might best be remembered for the farcical but grotesque death of his bride, who sloped off from a dull parade to smoke a crafty cigarette, caught fire and burned to death. As it is, he is celebrated as a prototype ecologist thanks to his avid defense of the Mallorcan flora and fauna, which he described in a nine-volume book <u>Die Balearen</u>. For more information about this unlikely eco-warrior, see www.ludwig-salvator.com.

Despite a hundred year history of environmental militancy, many Mallorcan species are still under threat, notably the Mallorcan Midwife Toad and (pictured) the Spur-Thighed Tortoise.

Time was when Polish migrants enjoyed a more romantic reputation than they do now. Forget plumbing and construction; think passion and revolution. In days gone by when the domestic needy were obliged to do the dirty jobs and keep the nation running, there was something decidedly exotic about the Poles. Take Chopin, for instance. Moody, melancholy and doomed, he was a tubercular refugee, didn't like work, declared himself to be a perfectly useless human being, and he shacked up with a cross-dressing controversialist with a false name. He wouldn't have got across many frontiers nowadays, but when he pitched up in Paris in the 1830s, he was the darling of the age, "the poet of the piano", taken up by cultural icons as diverse as Victor Hugo, Delacroix, Liszt, Berlioz and, of course, the trouser wearing George Sand. And it was she who brought him to **Mallorca** in a last ditch effort to save his lungs with a dose of the island's famously dry air.

Unfortunately, the couple encountered an unusually inclement winter that nearly killed the composer, and they were none too impressed with the Mallorcans, either, not least the medical men summoned by a despairing George Sand. "Three doctors have visited me," complained Chopin. "The first said I was going to die, the second said I was breathing my last, and the third said I was already dead". Doubtless there were good reasons for declaring the patient moribund, yet he survived for another ten years.

La Cartoixa

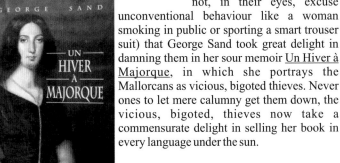

Lodging in a couple of monk's cells in **Valldemossa's** *La Cartoixa*, Sand and Chopin were miserable, damp and cold during their three month stay on the island, and were confronted by a local population who were so perfectly indifferent to the importance of their celebrity guests (an importance that did not, in their eyes, excuse unconventional behaviour like a woman smoking in public or sporting a smart trouser suit) that George Sand took great delight in damning them in her sour memoir Un Hiver à Majorque, in which she portrays the Mallorcans as vicious, bigoted thieves. Never ones to let mere calumny get them down, the vicious, bigoted, thieves now take a commensurate delight in selling her book in every language under the sun.

For the British, **Deià** must be the best known village in **Mallorca**, its name writ large by the association with Robert Graves, and the chances are that when you're wandering about the backstreets the first language you'll hear is English, often as not spoken by resident expats as visiting tourists and literary pilgrims. It's not my favourite place on the island, having become just that little bit too perfect, a tad too well preserved, a sort of museum town in the manner of somewhere like Florence, but as with all those places that appear to have been frozen in time by the heritage industry, it is at once an extraordinary site and an extraordinary sight.

Cala de Deià

Squeezed between soaring cliffs and the deep blue sea and surrounded by immaculately maintained terraces of silver green olives, the village itself clinging to a small knoll as if it was in danger of slipping into the sea, **Deià** is definitive picture postcard stuff, and the beach at the *cala* is a lovely place for a bathe, which is unusual for the northwestern quarter of the island, where most of the coves are better suited to boats than bodies.

Moreover, my prejudices notwithstanding, I don't doubt that there's more in the way of a traditional, communal life in **Deià** than meets the eye. When we were last there, for instance, there was a mimeographed

Can Boi municipal notice dotted about the town's lampposts calling an extraordinary meeting to discuss the annual *matanza*, the traditional pig-killing festival when everybody lends a hand: first the pigs get slaughtered, then they're scraped down, strung up and butchered, then the men get slaughtered while the women get on with the real work of preparing sausages and hams and black puddings and brawn and chitterlings and so forth. Somehow I doubt it's the expats who are elbow deep in blood.

Three particularly appealing features for the long distance walker:-
- the excellent **Hotel Es Molì**, a long-established favourite among the walking community;
- **Can Boi**, the first refuge en route, unless **Coma d'en Vidal** has opened in the meantime;
- *Autoservicio*, the self-service general store that's . . . well, I don't really know what to say. If the shop in **Estellencs** is *un poc de tot*, this is simply *tot*, everything crammed into an incredibly tiny space. You may have to check the sell-by-date if you're there out of season, but otherwise it's highly recommended. They sell good bread, too.

Un Hiver à Majorque is sold so widely on the island in so many languages one might be forgiven for supposing it the sum total of Mallorca's contribution to world literature, but the island is not without less bitter literary associations.

Ramon Lull, the thirteenth century Mallorcan mystic and philosopher wrote the first major work of Catalan literature Blanquerna, in which the eponymous hero overcomes various worldly temptations in his quest to become a hermit, only to be elected pope for his troubles - there's no justice in life, is there? Miguel Unamuno, the Basque academic and modernist who was a prime mover in Spanish literary circles between the Belle Époque and the Falangist coup, wrote an extended essay evoking the beauties of the island entitled En La Calma de Mallorca. The Catalan author and post-impressionist painter, Santiago Rusiñol, was so taken with the island, he dedicated an entire book to a similar theme, La Illa de la Calma. Gertrude Stein spent the spring of 1915 outside **Palma**, Anaïs Nin lived in **Deià** and wrote a short story about the place, the Nicaraguan poet Rubén Darío stayed -albeit briefly- in **Valldemossa**, apparently sleeping in a monk's habit and drinking so heavily that his hosts felt constrained to kick him out, and Jorge Luis Borges spent several of his formative years in the same town; but the author best known to British readers must be Robert Graves, the poet who twice won popular recognition, first with his early autobiography Goodbye to All That, then with the seminal toga-saga I, Claudius.

Graves first settled in **Deià** in the late 1920s with his wife, the poet Laura Riding, but was obliged to leave during the war years, returning in 1946 with his second wife, Beryl Hodge. The Graves' household attracted a wide variety of guests, ranging from Ava Gardner, Alec Guiness, and Peter Ustinov to a ten year old, stink-bomb wielding Stephen Hawking, but for obvious reasons it was above all literary figures who were drawn to **Deià** by Graves' reputation. Gabriel García Márquez, Kingsley Amis, Alan Sillitoe, Edna O`Brien, Richard Hughes, and Anthony Burgess all visited at one time or another, Burgess contriving to get himself assaulted by a bunch of hippies then beaten up by an American voodoo gang.

Stories about the eccentricity of Graves and his visitors are legion and often so bizarre one suspects they must be apocryphal, yet others are beyond invention. One journalist reports that the nurse who took care of the poet in his final years claims his last words were, "You're fired!" As exit lines go, it's almost as good as Spike Milligan's tombstone inscription: "I told you I was ill". Milligan, by the by, was another of Graves' friends. Their letters have been collected and published under the title, Dear Robert, Dear Spike.

Cala de Deiá

La Muleta from Cala de Deiá

views west from Ben d'Avalls lane

gnarled olive tree

Port de Sóller

Ofre & Es Cornadors seen from Sóller

waypoint 5

Muleta refuge

The official Stage Five of the *Ruta de Pedra en Sec* is both one of the easiest and the shortest by a long shot, a consequence, I suspect, of the simple fact that there was already a refuge in the old telegraph post at **Muleta**, the *Consell* had built one at **Deià**, and they didn't have any plans to build another between **Sóller** and **Tossals Verds** - ergo, it's a stage!

This may seem like a rather arbitrary way of breaking up a long-distance path, but the brevity is no bad thing, since it means we have a relaxed day after the rigours of Stage Four and plenty of time to stock up in **Sóller** or **Port de Sóller** prior to the biggest climb on the route. Better still, we no longer have any doubts about the itinerary. From here to the end, the GR is well-established and uncontested, the paths are all clearly sign and wayposted, and the book can be safely packed away after a preliminary perusal of what awaits us on the remaining stages.

The walk between **Deià** and the **Sóller** valley is, apart from one baffling stretch on the MA-10 (Wps.8-9 - it's hard to believe the authorities failed to negotiate a right-of-way using the various paths and terraces alongside the road), a pleasure throughout, following cobbled trails and attractive paths along terraces, through woodland, and over the rough, degraded terrain of the **Muleta** plateau, with fine sea views and our first clear perspective on the Tramuntana's main summits. Given the stage's overall easiness, I have taken the liberty of extending this day to **Sóller** town on the assumption that most people will want to push on as far as possible prior to the longer and more arduous Stage Six.

NB The 'Cala Deià' signposted route descending to the left from in front of the refuge is an attractive option for reaching Wp.5 more directly. See map.

5. Deià to Sóller including Muleta spur

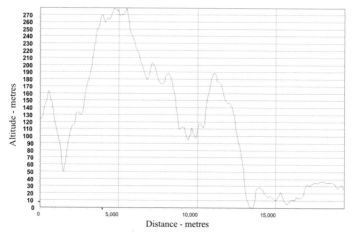

From the **Can Boi** refuge (Wp.1 0M), we take the one-way street climbing alongside the **Torrent des Racó** to the west, turning left after 150 metres into 'Calle Es Teix' (Wp.2), then carrying straight on after 30 metres on the pedestrianized 'Calle na Topa', which leads into the old village's main street. After passing the post-office, we descend to the left of 'Can Blau' to the MA-10, where we fork left on the 'Camí de sa Vinyeta' (Wp.3 8M), a tarmac lane descending toward the primary school.

NOTE: If you want to pop into the *Autoservicio* mentioned in the town sketch, bear right at 'Can Blau' then follow the MA-10 to rejoin the described route at Wp.3.

At the end of the lane, we go through a gate (Wp.4 11M) and follow a broad trail zigzagging down across terraces of olive trees, currently maintained by

Torrent des Racó

municipal sheep

what appear to be municipal sheep. The *camí* crosses the **Cala Deià** road three times before joining it 30 metres short of the 'Camí de Ribassos' footbridge, immediately in front of which, we climb to the right (Wp.5 22M).

Following a broad trail, we climb steadily out of the **Torrent Major/Cala de Deià** gorge. 150 metres after the path levels out, we veer right (Wp.6 29M) and climb gently to join a dirt track, on which we maintain direction (NE). 100 metres later, we fork right to pass behind a small byre (Wp.7), immediately after which we bear left to cross a cattle grid at the lower end of a surfaced lane.

Toward the top of the lane, ignore the little stub of wayposted trail climbing to the right (it only adds 25 metres to the road walking and lands you in the middle of a particularly hair-raising bend) and stay on the lane to join the MA-10 (Wp.8 36M), which we follow to the left. After 400 metres, we turn right on a stepped trail signposted 'Camí de Castello' (Wp.9 40M).

The trail runs into a lane 50 metres later. Following the wayposted route, we climb steeply until the lane veers right and passes behind the garden and swimming pool of 'Can Rosel', where we turn left (Wp.10 44M) on a broad dirt trail (blocked by fallen trees at the time of writing, but this is a popular itinerary and I'm sure it will be cleared by the time you read this). After a short but steady climb, the path levels out briefly and we see the western cliffs of **La Muleta**, where the next refuge is located.

A succession of long, shallow steps takes us onto higher ground where the path is flanked by a series of cabins and small houses, the most substantial of which, **Son Coll** (Wp.11 61M), abuts directly onto the path. A long, recently paved stretch (slippery when wet) brings us down to a junction with a dirt track and, to the left, a signposted path for 'Font de ses Mentides' (Wp.12 63M). Bearing right, we recover the old cobbled trail as it climbs to cross a tiny lane (Wp.13 66M).

After a pleasant stroll along a shady woodland terrace, the trail dips down to ford a watercourse then climbs briefly before a final level stretch brings us back into a more classic cultivated landscape of olive, oleaster and

threshing circle above waypoint 14

carob tree terraces. Passing behind a large threshing circle and shallow *aljub*, we drop down to join a dirt track (Wp.14 86M) on which we bear right, descending to a large eighteenth century farmhouse, commonly known as **Can Prohom**. In fact, **Can Prohom** is only the eastern wing of the house. The western wing, **Son Micó**, is a guest house serving coffee and orange juice, and some very tempting looking tarts.

Crossing the courtyard in front of the main building, we stroll down a cobbled trail to a derelict chapel (Wp.15 89M), where we turn left and descend to the MA-10 in front of the **Son Bleda** Hotel bar/restaurant (Wp.16 93M).

Son Micó

NOTE: If you're staying in **Sóller** and want to descend directly, the town can be reached by pleasant sign and wayposted routes carrying straight on at Wp.15 to reach the *Camís des Rost*, *Monts Reals*, *Rocafort* and *Castello*, or via the *Camí de Son Sales*, which begins behind the **Son Bleda** car-park and rejoins the GR at Wp.35.

Turning left and taking great care (there's a nasty little bend ahead), we follow the MA-10 for 125 metres then turn right on the 'Bens d'Avall' lane (Wp.17). When the main lane climbs slightly then descends sharp left some 600 metres later, we turn right on a track (surfaced for the first 50 metres) (Wp.18 105M). Bearing right (Wp.19) then left (Wp.20 109M) at the next two junctions, we wind through olive groves, individual trees looking so gnarled and ancient you can well believe some have been carbon-dated BC. Reaching a *'Camina per Mallorca'* mapboard, we either turn left for the **Muleta** refuge or carry straight on for 'Port de Sóller' (Wp.21 118M).

The spur to the refuge (of limited interest unless you're staying there), climbs briefly then traverses the **Muleta** plateau proper, an abandoned field of ancient olive trees. After going through a gap in a wall (Wp.22 6M from Wp.21), we leave the plateau, descending amid abundant *carritx* and equally abundant old blue-and-green waymarks on very rough, haphazard cobbling into fire-ravaged terraces overlooking **Port de Sóller**, where we fork left at a Y-junction (Wp.23 16M) (it looks like the right hand branch is going to be fenced off shortly). We then curve round a tiny cistern with a window-like vent and traverse a small rise before passing a limekiln. Thereafter, a straightforward descent bring us to a signposted crossroads (Wp.24 28M), where we carry straight on to reach the refuge 150 metres later (Wp.25 31M).

If you're staying at the refuge, you can either retrace your steps to Wp.21 (recommended), or descend via the road to **Port de Sóller**. In the latter case, to recover the GR, turn inland at the Bar Las Delicias II to pass the Campo Sol restaurant. The derelict Hotel Rocamar is on the right 300 metres later. The rough track cutting across its premises joins the GR at Wp.32.

Muleta Refuge

To reach Port de Sóller and Sóller from Wp.21, we maintain direction (E), carrying straight on at a crossroads 75 metres later (Wp.26) then forking right 25 metres after that (Wp.27) on a wayposted path that coils round the **Muleta de Cats Avinyons** farmhouse. Behind the farmhouse, we turn sharp left on a narrow path (Wp.28 123M not counting the **Muleta** spur) into another ancient olive grove.

Following a broad trail peppered with cairns, we join a cobbled way that dips into a swale then traverses a rise where views open out over **Port de Sóller**. Passing the **Muleta de ca s'Hereu** *agroturismo* farmhouse (offering orange juice and *pa amb oli* - bread and olive oil) (Wp.29 131M), we trace a horseshoe curve round the next gully then descend to go through one more olive grove (Wps.30-31 138M-141M), after which a good cobbled trail brings us down to a signposted junction behind the derelict Hotel Rocamar (Wp.32 149M).

curving round the gully after wpt 29

Forking right at the next junction (Wp.33 154M), we soon go through a gate to follow a terrace path behind a private house. After climbing briefly below cliffs so heavily mottled they look like they've been camouflaged, we descend

approaching the Son Sales valley

into the **Son Sales** valley, bearing right when our path feeds into a dirt track (Wp.34 166M) leading to a narrow tarmac lane (Wp.35 169M), the 'Camí de Son Sales'.

Turning left, we pass the **Hotel Ca n'Aí** and follow the lane till it ends a kilometre later (Wp.36 171M), where we again have a choice of routes. NB If you're new to walking in **Mallorca**, it's worth looking up at the mountains behind **Sóller** as you stroll along this lane. The horn like mountain on the right is **Es Cornadors**. To its left, the conical summit

Ofre & Es Cornadors

with a green fringe of trees and a small tonsure of exposed rock is **Ofre**. The **Barranc de Biniaraix**, which we climb in Stage Six, is the gorge between these two mountains.

At the end of the *Camí de son Sales*, the GR turns right, then left on a minor road leading to the by-pass. There are GR signs everywhere in **Sóller**, sending you all over the shop - quite literally; which is great if you want to buy something, but a bit frustrating if you're not having an IKEA moment. After all, I don't suppose many people do a long-distance path for the shopping opportunities! Hence our alternative way across town, 'round the houses' rather than 'all over the shop'. It's quieter, quicker, quainter, and avoids the narrow alleys of the town centre where 'kerb-crawling' takes on an altogether different meaning.

<u>**Round the houses:**</u>
Turning left, we cross the by-pass 100 metres later into 'Vial 68 Pont d'en Barona' (Wp.37), a partially surfaced track that drops down to run alongside the **Torrent Major**. After going through a pedestrian tunnel under a road bridge (Wp.38 177M), we cross the tramlines then turn left 100 metres later on a footbridge (Wp.39 179M) into the 'Camí de Can Guida', a path that promptly broadens to a lane lined with orchards and old houses. The lane winds through a couple of chicanes then, after 100 metres on the straight, we turn right, immediately in front of House No.6, on a tiny concrete path (Wp.40 183M).

Turning left after another 100 metres (Wp.41), we walk alongside an old stone culvert (often overflowing onto the path after heavy rain) to reach the end of another lane. We stay on this lane (largely in the company of horses, chickens, guinea fowl and rabbits) as it swings round to the left to pass the Ca's Curial hotel and emerge on a main road (Wp.42 191M), where we turn right to reach the football ground 150 metres later (Wp.43).

<u>**All over the shop:**</u>
If supplies are your priority, it's best to follow the official, signposted route. Turning right at Wp.36 then left 75 metres later (Wp.44), we follow a minor road that joins the by-pass at a roundabout (Wp.45). Crossing the by-pass, we turn right, then fork left 100 metres later (Wp.46) onto the *Camí des Camp Llarg* (unnamed at this end).

NOTE: the second turning on the left off the *Camí des Camp Llarg* descends to Eroski, the largest supermarket in **Sóller**.

Otherwise, we continue along 'Camí des Camp Llarg' until it crosses Carrer Cetre (the Carrer Cetre name plaque has fallen off the wall, but it's the broad road with the 'Agrotec' outlet), on which we turn left (Wp.47), then right into the 'Camí de sa Mar' (Wp.48). Turning left at the top of 'Camí de sa Mar' (Wp.49), we follow 'Carrer de la Rectoria' into the central 'Plaça de sa Constitució'. The excellent Panaderia Lareña is immediately on the right when you enter the plaza.

Placa de sa Constitució

Shopping opportunities sated, we take 'Carrer de sa Luna' beside the BBVA bank on the far side of the plaza (Wp.50) (passing the Pastisseria Frau where the *coca* is particularly delectable), then turn left into 'Carrer de la Victoria 11 Maig' (Wp.51). Carrying straight on at the crossroads, we fork right at the bridge, signposted 'Piscina Municipal' (Wp.52). The football field is on the right, 300 metres later, at the junction with the **Fornalutx** road (Wp.43).

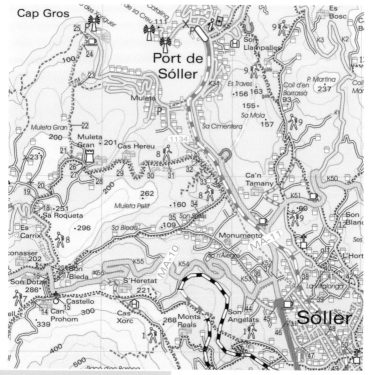

If you want to take a break midway through your walk, **Sóller** is the place to do it, not only because it is more or less the halfway point, but because it has the best services en route, good swimming at the Port, and is a pleasant place simply to stroll around, exploring the town's warren of paths, passageways and lanes, and discovering its varied buildings ranging from a couple of flamboyant even faintly pompous modernist institutional edifices to delightfully higgledy-piggledy houses pieced together, it would seem, room by room as finances allowed. Spending the best part of a month there writing up research and hiding from the sort of weather that did Chopin no good at all, we quite fell under the spell of the place. Surrounded by citrus groves and cradled by high mountains, it is all but designed to seduce, and only needs the pedestrianization of the town centre to perfect its charms.

Sóller's history has been defined by two apparently contradictory phenomena, the one its long-standing isolation from the rest of the island, which was only really ended by the construction of the road tunnel to the South in the 1990s (though economic isolation had effectively ended with the train tunnels engineered at the beginning of the twentieth

the tram crossing Plaça de sa Constitució

century), the other being expatriation and the subsequent return of migrant workers with a pocketful of cash and a head full of dreams.

You only need to glance at the surrounding ring of mountains to appreciate that in times past local people didn't get out and about very much, because you'd need a fairly compelling reason to undertake the gruelling climb involved in going just about anywhere except out to sea, and the slightly inward looking, self-sufficient nature of a community constrained to autonomy by circumstances is still palpable in **Sóller**, despite its recent success as a base for outward bound tourists. Some of the large, old houses in the town centre are almost Arabic in concept if not

looking for a way out of Sóller

in style, turning blank faces to the street, but concealing behind the facade an elaborate refuge for family and friends, and even the one-way system dictated by modern day traffic is so labyrinthine it suggests a turning away from the outside world, as if the secret heart of **Sóller** is something the townsfolk want to protect from facile intrusion.

However, economic realities tend to get in everywhere, no matter how well guarded, and in the second half of the nineteenth century the 'fairly compelling reason' alluded to above presented itself in the form of phylloxera. **Sóller** had had close ties with France ever since affluent fugitives from the French Revolution took refuge in the town, so when the region's vines were wiped out by sap sucking aphids and the local wine industry went, quite literally, down the tubes, it seemed only natural that Mallorca's newly indigent smallholders should decamp to France in search of work, the proceeds of which were subsequently invested in the orchards of oranges and lemons for which the valley is famous nowadays.

The pattern continued and, often as not, when you start chatting to someone from **Sóller**, you won't have to dig too far to discover a French link. **Son Micó** and **Can Prohom**, for example, which are well known to anyone who has visited **Mallorca** for a walking holiday, were purchased by the uncle of the present owners when he returned from working in France. The francophone association in **Sóller** boasts some 400 members and to this day a distinction is still made between the people who stayed and the *'Mallorquines de Francía'*.

Port de Sóller is an unpretentious low-rise resort with a pleasant seafront, a superb natural harbour, and a decent swimming beach (**En Repic** at its western end). There's some distressing looking construction activity creeping up the hillsides on either side of the harbour, but for the present it remains a good place for a bathe and a bite to eat. If you're staying in **Sóller** itself, the tram ride down to the seafront is a must.

Despite my strictures about the 'all over the shop' route taken by the GR to cross **Sóller** town, it must be said that there's a certain logic to their itinerary, since even if you're not staying overnight, you'll probably want to stock up on supplies. A few pointers that might be helpful:-
- if you've acquired a taste for Mallorcan baking, which I sincerely hope you have, you should stop off at the Panaderia Lareña on the main square, or better still at the Pastisseria Frau on Calle Luna.
- the deli beside the Pastisseria Frau is dear but worth it.
- in the unlikely event that you're getting weary of getting away from it all and feel a compelling urge to communicate with the outside world, there are two *locutorios* in **Sóller** offering internet access, one on Calle Luna, the other in the tiny alley leading out of the main plaza in front of the Banco Santander.
- the alternative accommodation options here are more extensive than anywhere else on the GR221. Readers and local specialists have recommended the hotels Porto Sóller, Marina, Es Port, and Brisas in Port de Sóller. In Sóller itself, most rooms in the budget Hostal Nadal come, we were assured by an elderly lady I took to be the owner, *con baño* i.e. 'with a bath', no small consideration when you're walking, and those that don't are considerably cheaper.

Ofre & Es Cornadors

Es Cornadors & Cornador Petit

lavadero waypoint 12

Barranc de Biniaraix

Puig Major under snow

Gorg Blau

Pas Llis

Salt des Cans

The biggest single climb of the GR221, the most spectacular gorge, and a contender (alongside the *Camí de s'Arxiduc*) for the title of Mallorca's most famous path make this stage one of the highlights of the *Ruta de Pedra en Sec*. Rising steeply from the southeastern corner of the **Sóller** plain, the **Barranc de Biniaraix** is a wonderful melding of wood, water and rock immaculately modelled by nature then honed by meticulous terracing in the gorge's lower reaches and the superposition of a path so perfect one could be forgiven for thinking it some sort of stairway to heaven . . . which it is in a way, since in the past it was trod by pilgrims making their way to **Lluc**, the spiritual heartland of **Mallorca**.

However, this being **Mallorca**, the two thousand steps of the trail (no, I didn't count them, but I'm willing to take it on trust) also served a very practical purpose, accessing the **Cúber** valley, formerly the locus of the summer transhumance when grazing was poor on the plain, and now the site of the island's largest reservoir. It's a glorious place with a real high mountain' feel to it and the basin of the **Ofre** farm, the estate dating back to Moorish times that we cross between the *barranc* and **Cúber**, is ringed by one of Mallorca's wildest rockscapes.

The only slight drawback here is that the **Cúber-Sóller** stretch of the stage is very popular with guided hiking parties who get dropped off at the top and do it as a linear descent, so be prepared: whilst you're toiling up the trail sweating freely and slowly turning the colour of a well-boiled beetroot, there's every possibility that you will be passed by parties of sprightly septuagenarians gaily dashing down the mountain merrily dishing out the *'Guten tags'* like they're going out of fashion.

The fact that we split this stage into two, the first part being the ascent to **Cúber**, the second the approach to the **Tossals Verds** refuge, is not merely symptomatic of congenital laziness. Congenital laziness may have played its part, but the principal motive was practical: we were camping, not staying at the refuges and, since I wanted to give readers the option of taking the more direct (and more demanding) **Pas Llis** route to the refuge, it seemed logical to split the stage and record the **Tossals Verds** paths separately.

Though an established favourite with holidaymakers, the **Tossals Verds** massif can be a surprisingly wild place, especially if you venture off the conventional itineraries, but it is notable above all for a nigh on flawless marriage of immediate gratification and grandiose vistas, boasting picturesque paths, pellucid springs, silvery torrents, breathtaking crags, beautiful woodland, and a panorama across the southern plain encompassing the two great sugar loaf mountains of **Alcaldena** and **Alaró** that is unique on the GR221. It also gives us a glimpse of one of Mallorca's most dramatic man-made walking monuments, the **Canaleta de Massanella**.

The only shortcoming of the **Tossals Verds** route chosen by the makers of the GR is that they do a bit of a Grand Old Duke of York, marching us all the way round the mountain to reach the refuge then pretty much all the way back again to begin the next stage. I can understand why. The path they've chosen is clear, easy, and presents no significant problems or risks of any kind; the alternative isn't and does, though the hazard is nothing like as great as the snapshots suggest. Which route you choose is a question of different strokes for different folks: if security and ease outweigh a slight potential for monotony, you should follow the standard route; if novelty and drama are your thing . . . well, read on.

The **Pas Llis** or 'Smooth Pass' featured in our alternative ending to this stage is a bit of a humbug when it comes down to it. Like one of those formidable Hollywood Grande-Dames with a fearsome reputation or some preening macho 'personality' who likes to pretend he's a real tough guy, it photographs well, but when you actually meet it, it's a lot smaller and less impressive than you had imagined.

Essentially, it is nothing more than a zig and a zag along two traverses with a plastic covered cable set into the rock as a handrail. The zig is about three metres long, between one and two metres wide, and climbs above a three-metre drop. The zag is five to ten metres long and wide enough to mask the overhang. Pathfinding is not a problem and the height shouldn't be a problem (personally, I get giddy just watching mountaineering documentaries, but I skipped along here with all the insouciance, if not the elegance, of a mountain goat), though adopting the precautionary principle, I have given it a vertigo warning.

Nevertheless, the alternative takes us into fairly rough, little visited terrain, so it does call for prudence and is only really recommended for experienced walkers. In particular, it's worth noting that we walk below some rather rugged cliffs that are clearly given to demonstrating just how rugged they are by dropping the odd rock on the path. Best not to venture onto the alternative after heavy rain or in high winds.

* in Biniaraix

6A. Sóller to Cúber

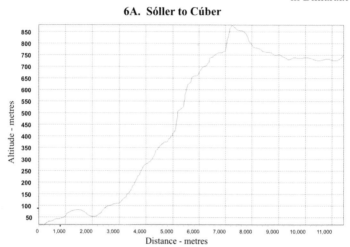

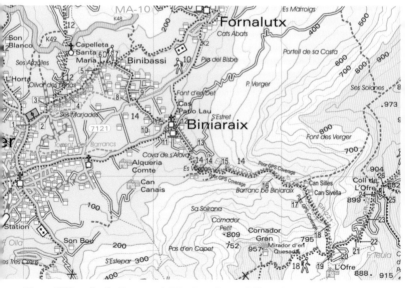

From **Sóller** football ground (Wp.1 0M), we follow the 'Fornalutx' road for 200 metres then turn left at a *'Camina per Mallorca'* mapboard onto a minor lane (Wp.2). We stick with the lane when it swings right 100 metres later at a junction with a surfaced track (Wp.3) and ignore a track forking off to the left after another 200 metres, when the lane becomes the 'Camí de s'Ermita' (Wp.4 7M). Directly ahead of us is Mallorca's highest mountain, **Puig Major**, which is largely off limits due to the military installations on the main summit.

house shortly before waypoint 5

At the end of the lane (Wp.5 15M), we turn left then right 30 metres later (Wp.6) on a narrow cobbled path climbing to the lovely little hamlet of **Binibassi**. In the heart of the hamlet, the path becomes a lane again (Wp.7 20M) that we follow down to rejoin the **Fornalutx** road, where we turn left (Wp.8 29M) then right at the bus-stop 50 metres later (Wp.9) into the 'Camí Horta de Biniaraix', another narrow lane that leads to a cobbled trail (Wp.10 34M) climbing into the village of **Biniaraix**.

Turning left on the village's minuscule main road (Wp.11 37M), we follow 'Carrer de Sant Josep' round to the old *lavadero* and the start of the 'Barranc de Biniaraix' dirt track (Wp.12 39M), where they suggest (with improbable pessimism given the mad antics of many Mallorcan ramblers) that it's going to take over four hours to reach

Lavadero

Cúber! It ain't, not unless we take it very easy indeed and make a point of stopping to elucidate the precise nature of all those *guten-tags*.

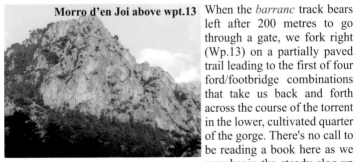
Morro d'en Joi above wpt.13

When the *barranc* track bears left after 200 metres to go through a gate, we fork right (Wp.13) on a partially paved trail leading to the first of four ford/footbridge combinations that take us back and forth across the course of the torrent in the lower, cultivated quarter of the gorge. There's no call to be reading a book here as we now begin the steady slog up those two thousand steps, so it's simply a question of following the paved trail and pausing from time to time to take in the views unfolding behind us. The following text is simply for the purposes of pacing progress and giving you an idea of what to expect.

'the Barranc trail'

S'Estret

Ignoring two paths off to the right (Wp.14 & Wp.15 52M), we climb steadily amid a riot of rock, carob, olive and oleaster, the gorge narrowing the higher we go and offering an increasing number of tempting little plunge pools. After climbing alongside an ancient aquifer, currently being relined with clay tiles, we go through the narrow **S'Estret** declivity and cross a stone bridge (Wp.16 73M), then recross the torrent 100 metres later via the third ford/footbridge combination.

After passing two small houses, **Can Silles** and **Can Sivella** (you wouldn't want to forget the bread, would you?

'Stepping Stone' ford

You may occasionally see locals climbing with their 'shopping caddies', miniature tractors that the hapless shopper follows on foot at a pace that would frustrate a lethargic snail) (Wp.17 83M), the trail veers away from the torrent and zigzags up amid pine and oleaster, passing two impressive overhangs of water-streaked rock as a superb panorama over the **Sóller** plain opens out behind us. Eventually, the trail levels off below a third overhang and we go through a gate (Wp.18 108M) into the **Ofre** estate - don't be alarmed by the *'Toros Bravos'* sign . . . you'd have to be a very *bravo toro* to tackle all the hikers who come

'Bravo'

through here and the only bovines I've ever seen on the **Ofre** estate were a couple of uncommonly placid cows.

Compared to the stiff climb up the cobbled trail, we now enjoy an easy

Ofre

stroll into the main bowl of the **Ofre** estate, passing a signposted turning on the right for the 'Mirador d'en Quesada / Es Cornadors' (Wp.19 117M). Thereafter, though, we go through a second gate and the climbing resumes on a rough trail heading toward the unmistakable conical peak of **Ofre**.

Joining a dirt track at a bend (Wp.20), we maintain a northeasterly direction, following the track for 250 metres until it goes through a sharp left-hand bend. Immediately after the bend, we turn right (Wp.21 126M) then left 10 metres later (Wp.22) on sign/wayposted paths that climb steadily through mixed Holm Oak and pine woods. We

Coll de l'Ofre

cross the track (Wp.23 131M) then rejoin it (Wp.24 137M) for 20 metres,

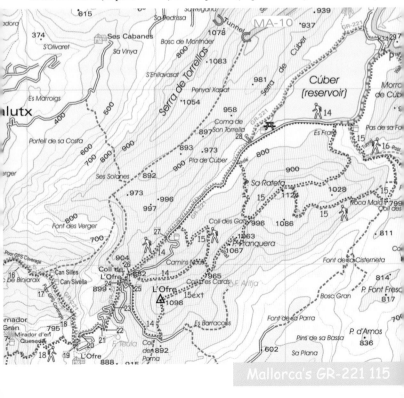

before recovering the path at a wayposted left hand turn (Wp.25) for the final climb to **Coll de l'Ofre**, where there's a large cross stuck in a pile of stones (Wp.26 140M).

Ahead of us we can see **Cúber**, the radar station on **Puig Major**, and to the right of the reservoir a rocky ridge formed by two distinct humps, the **Sa Rateta** and **Na Franquesa** summits. Beyond them, we can see **Puig de Massanella**, Mallorca's second highest mountain, which we traverse in the course of Stage Seven.

Carrying straight on, we follow a clearly sign and wayposted path toward the reservoir. After a gentle descent, the path joins the main **Ofre** track directly in front of the **Binimorat** farmhouse (Wp.27 150M). Turning left, we follow this track to the reservoir, where we fork left to go through a gate (Wp.28 167M) and follow the raised embankment round the northern shore, circling the reservoir to reach the main access gates at its eastern end (Wp.29 193M).

If you're undecided as to which path to take to reach **Tossals Verds**, when you're about halfway along the reservoir, more or less opposite the dam wall, look up toward the east and you will see a sweep of green dropping down from a broad rocky outcrop. The outcrop is the **Tossals Verds** massif, the rocky dip defining the near side of the green sweep the **Coll de sa Coma des Ases**, which we cross in the alternative route. It looks a little daunting from this perspective, but like many climbs, it's harder on the eye than underfoot.

6B. Cúber to Tossals Verds
via Coll des Coloms (the official route)

2 🚶	⌚ 2 H	⟹ 5.3 km	🏔 ↗80m ↘230m	⟺	🍽 4*

* at Refuge

6B. Cúber to Tossals Verds

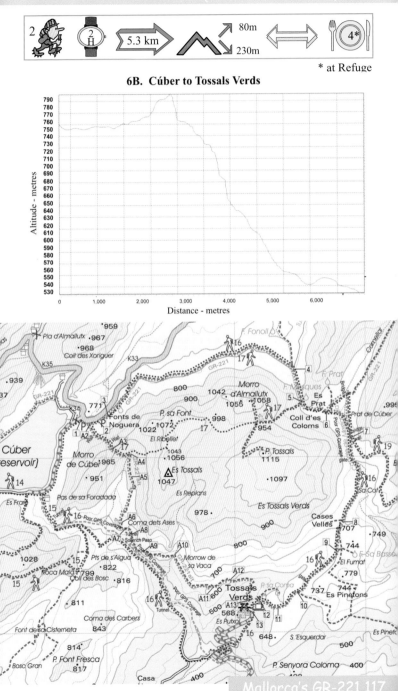

From the gates of the **Cúber** reservoir (Wp.1 0M), we follow the obvious, signposted path to the right along the inside of the main fence, crossing a stile into the **Font des Noguer** car-park a couple of hundred metres later (Wp.2). The spring and *área recreativa* are 100 metres directly ahead, otherwise we descend onto the road and bear right to reach a path signposted 'Font d'es Prat,

Gorg Blau

Refugi des Tossals Verds' (Wp.3 5M). From here we embark on a pleasant stroll alongside a modern, open, concrete canal, enjoying fine views over the **Gorg Blau** reservoir. The canal feeds **Cúber** with the overflow from **Gorg Blau**, despite the fact that the latter is the lower of the two reservoirs.

After passing three concrete ramps bridging the aquifer, we cross it via the fourth ramp (Wp.4 37M), and go through a wooden gate to climb steadily through the woods on a partially stepped and intermittently cobbled donkey trail. The trail levels out on the **Coll d'es Coloms**, where we pass a path off to the right (Wp.5 44M) and, 300 metres later, a turning on the left signposted 'Font des Prat 10m, Lluc 4h' (Wp.6 52M), the route followed in Stage Seven.

Carrying straight on, we continue on a broad trail descending between a couple of *sitjes* to a footbridge over the **Torrent des Prat**, just before which we cross the pipe bringing water to the refuge from the **Font des Prat**. Crossing the bridge, we pass directly below the renowned **Canaleta de Massanella** then, 75 metres later, recross the torrent via a ford set with stepping stones (Wp.7 57M). A brief climb brings us to a gate with a rather neat latch, after which we can see off to our left the somewhat startling arches of an aqueduct in the *canaleta*.

waypoint 7

a rather neat latch

Following a long, roughly cobbled stretch, we contour round the southern side of the **Tossals Verds** massif, enjoying fine views down towards **Mancor del Valle** and **Selva**. Emerging from the last scattering of Holm Oak into a drier landscape, we follow a smoother trail (SW), passing a signposted junction with a branch off to our right leading to the **Cases Velles** ruins (Wp.8 77M). Carrying straight on, we cross a broad *coll*, after which views open out over the **Cases Velles** valley off to our right.

Forking right at a Y-junction signposted 'Refugi 25m' (Wp.9 82M), we descend gently on a terraced path traversing rock and scrub. Going

waypoint 10

through a gateway, the descent steepens slightly as we pass one of the possible contenders for the title of **El Fumat** (see p123) . 150 metres later, we ignore a signposted turning for 'Mancor' (Wp.10 94M) and see another possible **El Fumat** (Wp.11 98M), 75 metres after which we get our first glimpse of the refuge. Descending past a restored charcoal burners' hut (though the restoration looked a tad precarious when we last passed) and a path off to the right to the 'Pou de sa Coma' (Wp.12 108M), we zigzag down a broad stony path to reach the refuge (Wp.13 112M).

the Refuge

3	2 H	4.8 km	150m / 410m	← →	3	4*

* at Refuge

6B alt. Cúber to Tossals Verds via Pas Llis

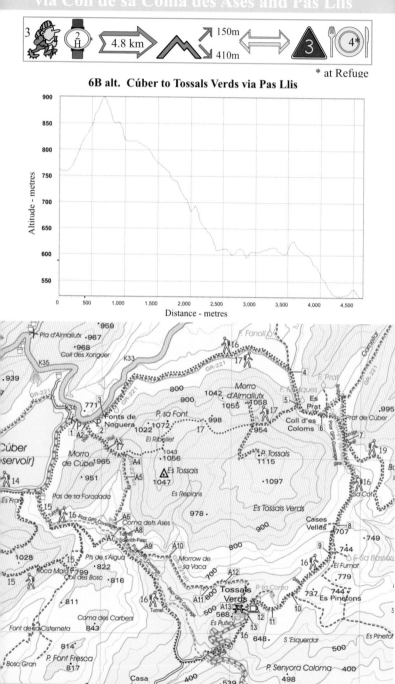

From the gates of the **Cúber** reservoir (Wp.A29/B01 0M), we follow the obvious, signposted path to the right along the inside of the main fence for a little under 100-metres, crossing the end of a broken wall beside the second of two fire-hazard warning signs, at which point we turn right, ignoring a GR waypost indicating that we carry straight on (Wp.ALT2). A rough path marked with cairns climbs steeply alongside the wall, then zigzags up via clear traverses to a gateway in another wall on the **Coll de sa Coma des Ases** (Wp.ALT3 21M) where views open out over the **Almedrá** valley toward the sugar loaf mountains of **Alcaldena** and **Alaró**, and we can see the continuation of our path winding along the eastern flank of the valley.

the wreck at waypoint Alt3

Descending steeply on a stony path, we cross the head of an affluent torrent, the **Coma des Ases** (Wp.ALT4 30M), where there are the remains of a wrecked light aircraft, though these are rapidly being consumed by the elements - five years ago, it was patently a plane, now it's merely the frame of a metal box. The path levels out here, crossing a small pass 250 metres later (Wp.ALT5 35M), after which it swings round to the right and we begin our descent toward the **Almedrá** torrent, on the far side of which we can see a covered aquifer, another classic link between **Cúber** and the **Tossals Verds** refuge (see 'Walk! Mallorca North & Mountains' Walk 16).

the Almedra Valley

Zigzagging down on the nearside of a band of rock, we pass to the left of a tiny ruin (Wp.ALT6 46M) then descend more steeply. The green fields visible at the end of the valley lie about a kilometre below the refuge. Within sight of one of the tunnels used on the aquifer route, the path levels out briefly to cross a long rockslide (Wp.ALT7 53M), but the steep descent soon resumes, heading directly toward the tunnel and the torrent. Shortly after crossing a second rockslide (Wp.ALT8 57M), a patch of path held in by a retaining wall squeezes behind a pine, bringing a second tunnel into view.

Passing below cliffs that bear a distant (possibly entirely fanciful) resemblance to the head of an elephant covered in carbuncles, we descend almost to the torrent, crossing a short, sloping outcrop of rock that's a

the bottom part of Pas Llis

Pas Llis

hands and bottoms job, after which a brief climb brings us to the base of the **Pas Llis**, where plastic covered cables fixed securely into the rock help us climb across the impressive but not manifestly dangerous pass (Wp.ALT9 66M).

The rough walking continues as we traverse exposed spines of eroded limestone and a slide of boulders, dipping up and down, and winding round the mountain below the glorious little crag of **Salt des Cans**, The Dogs' Leap! We then cross a second boulder slide composed of rocks so large and menacing you'll probably be skipping across them with all the agility, rapidity, and levity of a May Fly (it's certainly not the sort of place to hang about loudly declaring your atheism), 50 metres after which, at a point where an arrow and the word **Cúber** have been daubed on the rock in red letters (Wp.ALT10 77M),

Salt des Cans

we pass on our left an off-path route descending from between the **Salt des Cans** and **Morro de sa Vaca** (something along the lines of 'The Cow's Snout'). A little over half a kilometre later, we cross a small rise and get our first glimpse of the roof of the refuge on the far side of the **Es Putxol** spine of rock (Wp.ALT11 100M).

Heading east, we follow a smooth path intermittently invaded by *carritx*, contouring round the lower reaches of the **Cases Velles** valley, and gradually descending onto terraces of olive and oleaster, where we go through a gateway (Wp.ALT12 109M). Crossing the valley on a good dirt path, we come to a junction marked with a GR-waypost (not the main route, but a variant via the **Cases Velles** valley) (Wp.ALT13 116M), where we turn right to reach the refuge (Wp.13 120M).

the Refuge

El Fumat - Smoking Oaks & Pines

Dotted about Mallorca, there are a number of toponyms featuring derivatives of the word *fumar*, such as the impressive little peak of **El Fumat** on **Cap Formentor**, the **Camí de s'Alzina Fumadora** above **Fornalutx**, and (between Wps.9&11 of Stage 6B on the *Ruta de Pedra en Sec*) a large pine tree called **El Fumat**. It was only recently that I discovered these were all places where drovers, charcoal burners, and muleteers were wont to stop and have a fag, the **Cap Formentor** *fumat* being midway along the supply path between the **Cala Murta** dock and

El Fumat - maybe?

the lighthouse, the **Fornalutx** *alzina* being a large, shady oak at the head of the main climb, and the **El Fumat** on the GR221 being the largest pine tree in the area. Unfortunately, I've never quite established to my own satisfaction precisely which large pine is **El Fumat**, though there are plenty of places round here I'd gladly stop for a smoke. I'd always understood that the tree on the right at Wp.11 was **El Fumat**, but the one, also on the right, immediately after the gateway between Wps.10&11, or even the chopped up trunk on the left 175 metres after the gateway, both look pretty big and shady, making me doubt my original source. If anybody's carrying a tape measure or has a better eye than me for these things, I'd be glad to hear what you think!

Canaleta de Massanella

aquaduct on the canaleta

You've got to be careful what you say to a Mallorcan. Take, for instance, Montserrat Fontanet Llabrés, an eighteenth century pig farmer who really didn't take kindly to the fact that all the great engineers of the age confidently declared that it was 'perfectly impossible' to construct an aquifer between the **Font des Prat** and **Mancor del Valle**. Quite why they thought it was impossible in view of previous projects of a comparable nature undertaken by the Moors and Romans all over Spain, I wouldn't know, but whatever their pretext, be it financial, constitutional, or simply a question of competence, Sr. Llabrés was having none of it. He wanted his water down in the valley and he was blowed if a lot of feckless experts were going to tell him he couldn't have it, so he just went ahead and built the thing himself. And it's still in use today, not only for carrying water, but walkers, too. It has become one of the great adventure hikes on an island not short of adventure hikes and the perspective on the *canaleta* from Stages 6B/7A of the *Ruta de Pedra en Sec* ought to be enough to get most of you champing at the bit - in which case, I'm afraid you've got to buy another book! See 'Walk! Mallorca North & Mountains' Walk 19.

Puig Major

Serra de Teixos & Massanella

looking west below Coll des Prat

Tossals Verds - charcoal burners' cabin

Ses Voltes

Puig Roig

Coll des Telegraf snowpit

Son Amer refuge

For many visitors, **Massanella**, which we pass in Stage Seven of the GR221, is The Mallorcan Mountain, a definitive and unmissable experience, simply because it's the second highest and the highest accessible summit on the island, **Puig Major** being off-limits due to the military installations. To be honest, it's not my favourite mountain, largely I suspect out of irrational prejudice, but also because it's one where I've not always had the happiest of experiences.

First time I tried to record this stage, I was within a couple of hundred metres of **Coll des Prat**, that is to say had done most of the climbing and that in fairly filthy conditions, only to be chased off the snow-choked pass by driving glacial rain tending to hail, ending up back at **Font des Noguer** a couple of hours later a sodden, shivering wreck. It's not the sort of experience calculated to have you waxing lyrical about what a lovely little mountain this is.

Massanella - bad mood

Massanella - good mood

But in the end, those sort of difficulties and the challenges they embody are, of course, all part of the appeal of places like **Massanella**. Despite its very modest altitude, a mere 1365 metres (I know villages higher than that!), the proximity of the sea and the speed with which weather conditions can change in the Mediterranean, mean that Mallorca's most elevated peaks punch well above their height in meteorological terms, and can seem quite as wild and extreme as a two or three thousand metre summit on the continent.

Chances are you'll experience **Massanella** with blue skies and balmy temperatures that make 'high-mountain-warnings' sound risible, especially since the *Ruta de Pedra en Sec* culminates at a mere peck above 1200 metres. Nonetheless, at the risk of sounding a bit feeble, be warned: if you're going to experience potentially hazardous conditions on the GR221, it's probably going to be here. The old axiom of better-safe-than-sorry applies. If conditions look dangerous, return to **Cúber** and hitch a lift to **Lluc**. If they're turning so unpleasant that there's no point carrying on at all, descend from **Tossals Verds** to **Lloseta** or **Mancor** via the **Almedrà** valley or the signposted path at Wp.10 of Stage 6B.

Despite my prejudices though, I doubt many people will be disappointed by the penultimate day on the GR221. The climb to **Coll des Prat** features pleasant woodland and a wonderful prospect over the limestone summits surrounding **Cúber** and **Gorg Blau**, there's a real Pyrenean feel to the **Comafreda** valley, the views to west and east from the **Coll des Telégraf** are superb, the panorama from the **Puig d'en Galileu** balcony is one of the finest on the entire island, and the recently restored *Camí de Ses Voltes* trail is a gem.

Mention the *Ruta de Pedra en Sec* to a Mallorcan rambler and the chances are they'll laugh, possibly sneer, and on occasion be reduced to spitting fury, exasperated at its slow rate of progress and, according to some people I spoke to, scandalous misappropriation of money. Whether their outrage is justified or not, I wouldn't know, but whatever you think about the people responsible for the route, the work that has been done developing the refuges and restoring the **Ses Voltes** trail is beyond reproach.

The entire stage is beautifully wayposted, with tall wayposts installed on the northern side of **Coll des Prat** to ensure visibility after heavy snowfall. Too often in these sort of places one ends up anxiously glancing about, asking oneself, "Am I here? Am I there? What the bloody hell's that big bit of rock doing up there? That shouldn't be there!", but in this case the clear path and good wayposting mean we can, within reason, let our legs do the work and just follow our noses, concentrating instead on the unfolding sensory spectacle.

7A. Tossals Verds to Font des Prats junction

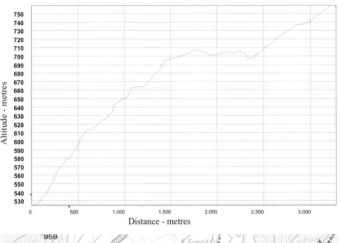

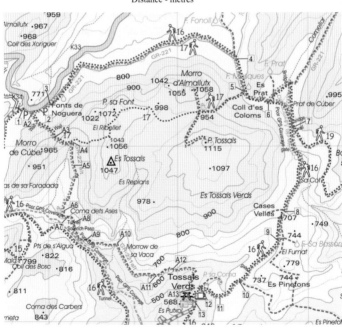

If you followed the conventional route of the GR to the refuge, retrace your steps to the **Font des Prat** turn-off, where our main description of Stage Seven begins. If you camped out at **Font des Noguer**, follow Stage

6B Wps.3-6 to the **Font des Prat** turn-off. If you did the alternative path via **Pas Llis**, here is a brief description of the course taken by the GR round the southern side of the **Tossals Verds** massif (Stage 6B Wps.12-6). See the description of the standard approach to the refuge for more details. Wp.6B11 is not mentioned because it is not relevant for pathfinding.

From the refuge (0M), we take the signposted path directly to the left of the main building for 'Font des Noguer 2h10, Font des Prat 1h10'. The broad, stony path climbs steadily, passing a signposted branch on the left for 'Pou de sa Coma' (Wp.12 6M), after which the gradient eases off as we approach the small conical summit of **Ses Cuculles** and the southern flank of **Massanella** comes into view.

Carrying straight on at an intersection with a signposted way down to 'Mancor' (Wp.10 18M), we go through a gateway in a wall, from where we can see the head of the **Cases Velles** valley and the ruins themselves on the left. We carry straight on again at junctions with a path doubling back to the right (Wp.9 31M)

Cases Velles

and the top end of the Wp.6ALT13 variant on the left (Wp.8 36M).

waypoint 9

After following a long, roughly cobbled trail, we eventually dip down to cross the **Torrent des Prat** via a ford (Wp.7 54M), 75 metres after which a bridge takes us back onto the torrent's right bank. We pick up the main stretch of Stage Seven 300 metres later beside a *'Camina per Mallorca'* mapboard, signposted 'Font des Prat 10m

Lluc 4h' (Wp.6 62M).

waypoint 6

* at Lluc

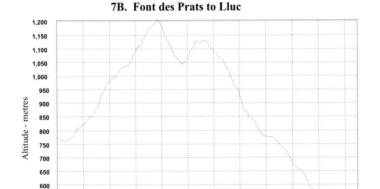

7B. Font des Prats to Lluc

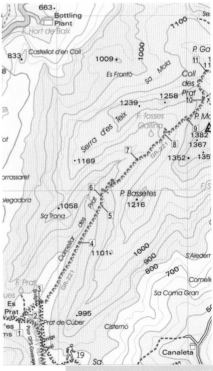

From the **Font des Prat** turn-off (Wp.1 0M), we follow a stony path (NE) that doubles as a torrent during wet weather. Going through a gateway in a wall and passing a sheepfold, we ignore a fork off to the left (Wp.2) and carry straight on, passing single and twin *sitjes* to reach a signposted junction at a footbridge 50 metres south of the **Font des Prat** (Wp.3 5M).

Carrying straight on for 'Coll des ses Cases de sa Neu 1h30', another name for the **Coll des Prat**, the *cases de neu* being the snowpits previously used for stockpiling ice, we cross the footbridge and continue on a clear path climbing gently through the woods. After a pleasant stroll through dense, mixed woodland, the landscape gradually changes, the pine and shrubs giving way to an underwood of boulders shadowed by mature Holm Oak, amid which the path levels out for 150 metres before passing a particularly large *sitja* and going through a gateway formed by the end of a wall and large blocks of rock (Wp.4 17M). We then resume climbing more steeply, the path begins to twist and turn to break the gradient, and the Holm Oak gradually give way to pine, between which we can glimpse the **Serra des Teixos** off to our left.

Font de ses Tosses d'en Gallina

Forking right at Y-junctions with two shortcuts within 100 metres of each other (Wps.5 26M & 6) between which we pass the **Font de ses Tosses d'en Gallina** spring, we emerge from the woods and the **Coll des Prat** comes into view directly ahead of us, framed by the rocky pinnacles of the **Serra des Teixos** and the

massive bulk of **Massanella**. Climbing steadily, we pass an off-path cairn-marked fork climbing on the right toward **Massanella** (Wp.7 34M) and the first fairly unimpressive - you could mistake it for a sheepfold if you didn't know what it was- snowpit (Wp.8 43M).

looking towards Coll des Prat

A second, cairn-marked off-path ascent of **Massanella** forks off to the southwest at the corner of a sharp left hand bend in the main path (Wp.9 52M), 275-metres after which we reach the **Coll des Prat** at a signposted junction beside a crumbling wall (Wp.10 56M). I would imagine the view is rather fine from here, unfortunately the *coll* was

Coll des Prat under snow!

engulfed in dense mist the day I passed and I couldn't see a thing!

Crossing the wall and bearing left for the 'Casa de Neu d'en Galileu 1h15', we follow a narrow path marked with prominent wayposts over a band of rough rock and descend past a second more substantial snowpit. The path,

second 'Snow-Pit'

still narrow but well-defined and clearly marked with cairns or waypoints, zigzags down into the spectacular **Comafreda Valley** toward the **Coll des Telégraf**, which is flanked by a couple of really striking snowpits, dug so deep and lined so neatly with tailored stone you begin to appreciate just how highly people used to value refrigeration for culinary and medicinal purposes.

Having enjoyed a superb outlook over **Puig Major** and the snaking progress of the celebrated **Nus de Corbata** road (the 'tie knot' since it actually tunnels under itself at one point) down to **Sa Calobra**, we turn right at the **Coll des Telégraf** (Wp.11 67M) and descend (E) past the largest snowpit yet along the right flank of the **Comafreda Valley**, enjoying fine views over the **Albufera** wetlands and **Alcúdia** bay. The

Comfreda valley

path doubles back to the left a couple of hundred metres after the snow-gathering ruins and we cross the dry **Comafreda** torrent (Wp.12 76M) to begin climbing toward the diminutive, but enchanting summit of **Puig d'en Galileu**.

A gentle to steady climb on a rocky path cutting a swathe through the *carritx* brings us to a waypost at an intersection with a path off to the right to **Puig d'en Galileu** (Wp.13 88M). Turning left, we enjoy one of the most astonishing spectacles yet as we stroll along a broad, *carritx* covered 'balcony' overlooking the gash of the **Torrent de Pareis** (Europe's second

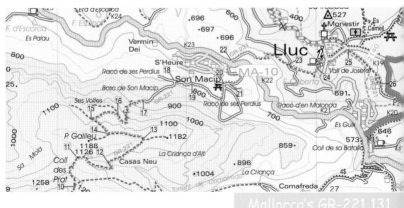

largest gorge) and the final sweep of mountains off to the east. The square building directly ahead of us, perched pretty much in the middle of nowhere to the right of the gorge, is the **Quartel de Carabiners**, an abandoned barrack dating back to the days when the wild northern coast with its harum-scarum *passos* was so popular with smugglers.

Quartel de Carabiners

Cami de Ses Voltes

Ignoring a minor, cairn-marked branch off to the left (Wp.14 95M), we descend (NW) to a signposted junction (Wp.15 99M) with a path accessing the well preserved 'Casa de Neu d'en Galileu'. Doubling back to the right at the junction, we head east to the edge of the **Galileu** balcony, where we reach the head of the magnificent *Cami de Ses Voltes* (Wp.16 105M), at which point the **Lluc** monastery comes into view. The path zigzags down toward the **Son Macip** wood, twisting back and forth so tightly it resembles terracing from above. The large mountain off to the right is **Puig Tomir**, which we skirt on the near side in Stage Eight.

Puig Tomir

The path continues its serpentine progress as we move down through the upper reaches of the wood, where it becomes a dirt track (Wp.17 121M) that winds downhill past *sitjes* so mossy you half suspect they're part of a lovingly tended lawn or perhaps a hobgoblin's bowling green. Ignoring a branch track doubling back to the left (Wp.18 128M) then carrying straight on 200 metres later when the main track swings left (Wp.19), we follow a contour for 400 metres. The contour track then dips into a gentle slope that takes us past a picnic table, immediately after which, we turn right on a narrow, wayposted path (Wp.20 137M) going through a gate to join a charcoal burners' cart track (Wp.21 138M).

looking NE from Ses Voltes

Turning left, we descend steadily to cross the MA-10 (Wp.22 145M), beyond which we follow a path (E) that soon broadens to a cart track descending gently through the woods towards **Puig Tomir**. 300 metres later, the track becomes a cobbled trail and the gradient steepens before eventually bottoming out beside a terrace path branching off to the left (Wp.23 158M). Carrying straight on, we follow the broad, wayposted trail until it emerges at a junction with the *Camí Vell de Lluc* (climbing from **Caimari** where the island's main pilgrimage routes converge) at the southwestern corner of the **Lluc** car park, beside the **Font Cuberta** (a spring said to be an excellent curative for stomach upsets) and the restaurant of the same name (reputation unspecified) (Wp.24 164M).

The monastery is directly ahead. The camping area is off to the right on the eastern side of the car-park. To reach the **Son Amer** refuge, we carry straight on, bearing right at the monastery gates to follow the access road toward the MA-10 for 150 metres, then turn right (Wp.25 170M) on a clearly signposted trail that reaches the refuge some 650 metres later (Wp.26).

I once heard a woman in Barcelona proudly announcing that the Catalans were the most elegant people in the world - tall, stylish, graceful, slender . . . I nearly fell off my chair. The people of the Catalan speaking lands have many qualities, but uncommonly elegant they are not, and the reason is simple: hearty peasant fare. **Mallorca** is no exception to this rule, in fact, I'd even suggest they push the boundaries a little further.

This, after all, is the home of *sobrasdada*, a pepper and pork pâté sausage that pops up just about everywhere in Mallorcan cuisine (spread, sliced, diced, fried, blended, stewed, stuffed . . . you name it, somebody's done it with *sobrasada*) and would doubtless have much the same impact on a modern dietician as a cross brandished in front of a vampire. It is, needless to say, delicious, above all if you can get hold of some of the home-made stuff. Equally tasty is *sopa Mallorquin* (a broth so thick that you could probably stand on it without sinking), which is composed of such a multitude of ingredients that one can spend an entire meal poking about and exclaiming at the delicious discoveries. In a similar spirit of chuck-it-all-in-and-mix-it-all-up, when faced with an excess of perishable offal after the annual pig-killing or *matança*, the Mallorcans opted for a damn good fry up, preserved on modern menus as *frit mallorqui*.

There is the odd fit of healthy eating and haute cuisine, such as *tumbet* (a variant on ratatouille) or *llom amb col* (pork, pine nuts and raisins wrapped in a cabbage leaf) or *arros brat*, 'dirty rice', the Mallorcan version of paella, but on the whole the Mallorcan diet is the sort of feast that you go on holiday to indulge in without having a doctor looking over your shoulder. Above all, it's ideal for walkers who have had a hard day up in the mountains getting their cardiovascular systems into trim and think (probably erroneously, but there you go), "Right, now I can really let myself go!"

Mind you, you might not have much of an appetite if you've started the day with *ensaimadas*, the stuffed pastry (most often filled with *cabello de àngel*, 'angel's hair' or shredded pumpkin, but occasionally with cream, apricot, or historically with the ubiquitous *sobrasada*) that is nowadays not so much a bun as a national institution, and have then gone onto picnic on Mallorcan pizzas (*coca*),

pasties (*cocarrois*) and pies (*empanada*), all of which are sold by local bakers. If you need to refresh your palate, the fresh orange juice (*zumo de naranja*) is superb, and you could do a lot worse for an appetizer than the excellent Mallorcan olives and almonds (*olivas/aceitunas* and *almendras*).

Mallorcan wines don't enjoy the international celebrity of those from the mainland like Rioja and Ribera del Duero, and probably never will given the territorial constraints, but the industry has recovered from the phylloxera plague of the 1890s that sent countless day labourers and small landowners into penurious exile, and a number of wines are highly prized by specialists. The best known denominations are Binissalem and Pla i Levant, but some good wines are also produced under the slightly dubious sounding title of *viña de la tierra*, many using indigenous varieties of vine like *moll*, *prensal blanc*, *callet*, *fogoneu*, *girò blanc*, and above all *manto negro*, a notoriously temperamental grape that one local wine-maker has fondly compared to a wild animal in need of domestication! The only drawback is that Mallorcan wines tend to be either pricey or dicey. For consistent and affordable quality we recommend Pere Seda Novell and the wines of Jose L. Ferrer, both of which are available in most supermarkets and grocers.

Need a digestive? *Carajillo* is coffee with a tot of brandy in it, *hierbas* a type of anisette, or you could try a glass of *orxata/horchata*, an almond milk that according to one legend got its name when Jaume I was offered a glass by a little girl who called it 'milk'; the king took one sip and promptly exclaimed *"Això no es llet. ¡Això es or, xata!"* - That's no milk. That's gold, sweetie!

Graceful and slender? Frankly, my dear, I don't give a damn.

When we first went to **Mallorca**, I was puzzled by the municipal boundary signs for **Escorca** because, as far as I could work out, apart from being a restaurant, a bus-stop and a border, the place didn't exist. I was right, too. Visit the *ayuntamiento's* website (www.ajescorca.net) then click on *historia* and you come up with a blank page. Escorca is a strictly administrative fiction, the 'town' hall being obliged to lodge itself within the walls of a religious foundation, but it hardly matters, because the natural and manmade phenomena that fall within the municipality are as interesting and significant as any more coherent urban nucleus.

Spot the 'Town'

On the natural side, we have the **Torrent de Pareis** (Europe's second largest gorge), the most spectacular of the karstic landscapes for which the island is so famous, several of Mallorca's highest mountains, plus the popular **Tossals Verds** massif, which shares its name with the estate dating back to the sixteenth century that is now a refuge. But it is the man-made things that are the particular focus of these mini-essays and the two that spring immediately to mind are seen during Stage Seven of the *Ruta de Pedra en Sec*.

Nus de Corbata

Mallorca has many remarkable roads, but probably the best known is the **Nus de Corbata** or Tie-Knot road descending to **Cala Tuent** and **Sa Calobra** at the seaward end of the **Torrent de Pareis**. This extraordinary bit of engineering takes the commonplace twists and turns of your average **Tramuntana** road and tightens them up a couple of notches, actually passing under itself at one point (hence the tie-knot), creating an outing that is definitely a gasper and can edge into white-knuckle-shrieking-out-loud territory if you make the mistake of going against the flow of tour buses, which descend at midday and return mid-afternoon. We only glimpse the flatter upper reaches of the road from the GR221, but if you have a day spare at the end of the walk or fancy an extra night at **Son Amer**, it's worth taking the public bus down to **Sa Calobra** (seasonal timetable) and spending an afternoon exploring the mouth of the **Torrent de Pareis**.

The bus also serves the other great manmade feature of **Escorca**, Mallorca's spiritual heartland, the **Lluc** monastery. The principal religious attraction here is **La Moreneta** ('the little dark-skinned one', the familiar Catalan name for a Black Madonna), a statue of the Virgin said to have been discovered, as these things are, by a *converso* shepherd boy. Themselves playing true to type in these stories, misguided prelates promptly shifted the thing into the local church, but it just as promptly shifted itself back again, which lead to a bit of tussle, **La Moreneta** zinging back and forth between Her chosen spot and the space allocated by the priests until the clerics gave up and built a shrine to house Her where She wanted to be. What became of the shepherd boy, I don't know, but it would seem his find was providential. *Lucus* had been a sacred wood to the Romans, was thereafter venerated by the Moors as *Al-luc*, and excavations have since proved it was also a Bronze Age burial ground. A stubborn statue with miraculous powers of locomotion was probably a very necessary device in the process of reclaiming the land from the Moors.

The story proved sufficiently potent to have pilgrims beating a path to **Lluc** from all over the island for the next 800 years, though not quite so potent it didn't require supplementing with new miracles from time to time. In the sixteenth century, a landowner cut off public access to the spring used by pilgrims and monks (*plus ça change*), whereupon the spring dried up and reappeared in its present position as the **Font Cuberta**. If only such problems were always so readily resolved! There are several paths in **Mallorca** that really ought to get their act together and move themselves.

To be honest, I'm not the best person to talk about **Lluc**, since I've always taken one look at its vast teeming car-park and swiftly bunked off into the hills, à la Moreneta, but it is a beautiful spot, and readers of our previous publications who have stayed at the monastery (closer to a good *pension* than a monastic retreat as I understand it, the 'cells' all being en suite, and the monastery itself housing several bars and restaurants) had good things to say about the experience. It's also worth visiting the Ca s'Amitger Tramuntana Information Centre (tel. 971-517-083) in the main car-park, where there's a permanent display about the island's flora and fauna, and an attendant who can tell you all you need to know about the mountains and meteorological conditions.

The Linea 5 bus to **Sa Calobra** leaves **Pollença** at 10.20, arrives in **Lluc** at 10.50, stops for an hour then reaches **Calobra** at 12.45. Departs for the return at 3pm, leaving **Lluc** at 4pm. A local website suggests passengers picking up the return bus from **Lluc** should be at the stop well in advance as the bus "doesn't hang about on the way back"!

Vultures rarely enjoy a loveable image in popular culture, and until recently, the Black Vulture population on Mallorca was no exception to this rule. Relying on the island's mountain livestock for the greater part of their diet, they were widely regarded as a pest, and by the early eighties the Black Vulture (also known as the Monk Vulture for its tonsure and cowl like ruff) had virtually been wiped out by poisoning.

Self-preservation was further complicated by the fact that this is the largest bird in Europe and one of the heaviest in the world (weighing up to 15 kilos), so very large and heavy that it needs a good breeze to get off the ground and plenty of thermals to remain airborne, as a result of which they are rarely seen in the morning. I've even heard tales of vultures stuffed so full of carrion that they were temporarily grounded, reduced to pedestrians while the process of digestion took its course, and consequently to be seen plodding along the roadside to return home from their feast. Indeed, in one notable instance, an exceptionally gluttonous vulture had consumed such immoderate quantities of a horse's carcass that it actually fell out of the tree where it had been enjoying a post-prandial nap, scaring the hell out of a couple of tourists who happened to be picnicking nearby.

Ill repute and ungovernable appetites notwithstanding, with changing values and the realization that **Mallorca** had one of the last breeding colonies left in Europe, a campaign was set up to save the Black Vulture, and it is now promoted as the emblematic bird of the Mallorcan mountains. Some farmers may still let slip the odd drop of poisoned bait, but for most people on the island, the Black Vulture population (which numbers about 80 now, four times what it was twenty years ago) is the source of considerable pride, and visitors who ignore restrictions designed to protect the birds' breeding habitat can expect very short shrift indeed. The best place to see these magnificent raptors on the GR221 is around the **Cúber** reservoir. Their main breeding ground is in the **Havanor** estate, north of the *Carretera Vella de Pollença* (Stage Eight - see 'Walk! Mallorca North & Mountains' Walk 34).

Other charismatic avians include Osprey, Eleanor's Falcons, Booted Eagles, Peregrine, Kestrel, Red Kite, Audouin Gulls, and Hoopoe. Start counting the migrants in with the residents and one's tempted to say that in **Mallorca** the sky's the limit: Terns, Bee-eaters, Hirundines, Marsh Harriers, Shrikes, Wheatears, Redstart, Stonechat, Whinchat, Bunting, Pipit, Crossbills, Goldcrest, Firecrest, Rock Thrush, Fantailed Warblers, Serins, Chiff Chaff . . . the list is endless and you could happily chant yourself into a trance reciting all the birds that can be seen. Dedicated twitchers should seriously consider extending their trip to spend a few days in the northeast of the island. The best months for combining walking and bird-watching holidays are April and May.

restored cabin at waypoint 8

Binifaldo & Puig Tomir

Font de Montanya torrent

views over Pollenca & Formentor

Puig Tomir

waterfall above Son Marc valley

Son Marc valley & Puig Maria

steps after waypoint 31

Despite the fact that it once involved trudging along six kilometres of tarmac, the *Carretera Vella de Pollença* at the tail end of the *Ruta de Pedra en Sec* has long been a favourite with holidaymakers who like their walking on the leisurely side, and it's easy to understand why. The old 'road', which in places is so very old that it's a cobbled trail dating back to Roman times, traverses some very lovely woodland, is framed by fine views of the most popular mountains at the eastern end of the **Tramuntana** (many of them only accessible on Sundays), takes us within a few hundred metres of some of Mallorca's finest karstic landscapes (see 'Walk! Mallorca North & Mountains' Walk 32 for a short detour off the G221), and yet puts minimal strain on our knees, nerves and hearts.

To top it all, no matter how laggardly the pathmakers may have been about developing the GR in the west, they've done us proud for our last day, renegotiating old rights-of-way to reduce the road walking (above all the dismal two kilometres on the MA-10 that used to blight the standard itinerary) to a minimum. They've also taken great care with sign and wayposting, so though the description may sound a bit complicated since this is very much a manmade landscape with no end of intersections, the book can be safely stashed once you're on path.

It's not grandiose walking (we've done grandiose already) and you can't really say the *Ruta de Pedra en Sec* ends with a bang, but it's certainly no whimper, being instead something in the order of a soft and pleasant murmur, bringing us down gently from the highs of the preceding week's walking, and easing us back into the lowland world from which we have briefly, but hopefully unforgettably, escaped.

Take your time, take it easy, and take your pleasure - we're going home!

* in Pollença

NB When you're descending from the refuge to the car park where our itinerary starts, don't be confused by the GR222 sign indicating the *Cami Vell* to **Caimari**, another LDP that is still in the project stage and likely to remain so for some time to come.

Behind the exceptionally large oak and a *'Camina per Mallorca'* mapboard at the southeastern corner of the main **Son Amer** car-park (Wp.1 0M), we take a broad trail alongside the MA-10, which we cross 100 metres later (Wp.2) to continue on a new path leading to a stony track, sometimes known as the *Cami de s'Ermita*. Traversing reclaimed land recently replanted with saplings (E), we go through a gateway in a wall (Wp.3 7M). Ignoring a branch off to the left immediately after the gateway, we carry straight on along a broad track climbing gently through

8. Lluc to Pollença

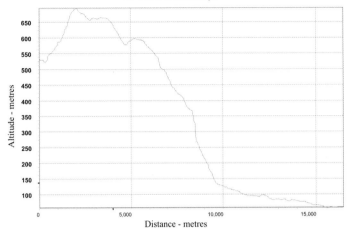

the woods.

The track eventually veers south to an intersection with another track, immediately before which, we turn sharp left on a narrow, wayposted path (Wp.4 17M) that doglegs round the restored, seventeenth century **Ermita de Son Amer** before rejoining the main track just above the 'Font de s'Ermita' (Wp.5 23M). Turning left, we continue climbing amid immaculately maintained oak wood, ignoring two branches off to the right (Wps.6&7) and a 'Mirador' signposted branch on

waypoint 4

the left (Wp.8 29M). 25 metres later, we fork right on a wayposted path (Wp.9) leading to a stile over a wall after a further 75 metres (Wp.10 32M).

waypoint 10

Pat yourselves on the back, purr softly to yourselves, smooth down your eyebrows with a moistened forefinger, break out a bottle of champagne, or do whatever you ordinarily do to display satisfaction with yourself because, apart from a couple of stiles and a rise so negligible you probably won't notice it, we have just completed the last climb on the GR221!

Ignoring a track descending to the right immediately after the stile, we cross the plateau of **Coll Pelat** (N) to reach a junction with a dirt track 130 metres later (Wp.11). The left branch descends to the publicly owned **Menut** farmhouse, but we bear right, maintaining altitude for the moment amid marvellously mossy mature oak. After going through a gateway, the track descends within sight of the western wall of **Puig Tomir** to reach an S-bend, at the top of which a waypost indicates where we leave the track, carrying straight on along a very narrow dirt path (Wp.12 46M).

The path becomes much clearer once we're on it, contouring round the **Moleta de Binifaldó** to reach the end of the access road at the gates of the former **Binifaldó** bottling plant, where the classic ascent of **Puig Tomir** begins (see 'Walk! Mallorca North & Mountains' Walk 31) (Wp.13 58M). If you need water, steps lead to a spring on the right 100 metres down the access road. Otherwise, we simply follow the access road (rarely busy, closed to traffic altogether at the weekends, and even tinged with moss in places, as if the forest has a fancy to reclaim the thing) for 700 metres, bringing into view the grand Sunday-only summits of **Puig Roig** and **Puig Caragoler de Femenia**, and passing some fabulous centenary oaks.

75 metres after the **Binifaldó** farmhouse, formerly the property of the Knights Templars after they'd nabbed it off Bini-Haldum (i.e. the Moorish 'sons of Haldum') and now run by the government as a *'Centre d'Educació Ambiental'*, we turn right on a signposted trail for 'Pollença 3h' (Wp.14 70M). We are now on the 'old road' proper, the bit that has always beguiled your more laidback walker, and you'll soon see

Carretera Vella

why. Frankly, it's the sort of 'road' that makes one hanker for the days when donkeys took precedence over cars and drivers who didn't employ a pedestrian with a flag to warn of their advent were considered an anti-social nuisance.

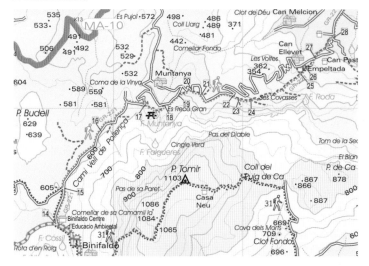

After crossing the **Binifaldó** pasture, we're soon back in the woods again, much of it so mossy one's tempted to call it mossland with a bit of wood scattered about for the purposes of decoration, though there are some outstanding mature oak. Passing a track descending on the left to the **Menut** *área recreativa* (Wp.15

'Mossland'

76M), we go through a gate (Wp.16 85M), from where we get our first glimpse of the sea to the west of the island. Ignoring all unmarked branches, we follow the main track as it descends gently, enjoying ever improving views over the bay of **Pollença** and the rugged peninsula of **Cap Formentor**.

The sail-like pinnacle off to our right at the tail-end of the **Tomir** massif is the **Cuculla de Fartarix**, the little hump to the right of **Pollença** is **Puig de Maria** and the large rise of rock off to our left is **Puig Gros de Ternelles**, the site of a celebrated and on-going right-of-way battle. The road climbing to the **Ternelles** martello tower, **Torre d'Ariant**, from near km5 of the MA-10 is public yet sealed off by a locked gate. Shortly before the present publication was being researched, local ramblers announced a mass 'trespass' to protest against the closure. Needless to say, on the day in question, the gate was open. Equally needless to say, the very next day it was locked again!

Font de Montanya stepping-stone

A little under a kilometre from Wp.16, we reach our first wayposted shortcut (Wp.17 94M), a restored stretch of the old cobbled trail recrossing the track less than 50 metres later. The descent gets steeper as we zigzag down beside the **Font de Muntanya** torrent (an ideal spot for a picnic), which we cross via a solitary stepping stone, immediately after which we rejoin the track (Wp.18 100M). Our second wayposted shortcut is via the middle branch of a triple junction 250 metres further on (Wp.19), rejoining the main track 50 metres later. Thereafter, the track twists back and forth through a series of tight bends and we take wayposted shortcut No.3 at the end of the long tail of the first chicane (Wp.20 107M).

Ignoring a minor branch doubling back to the left ten metres after we rejoin the main track (Wp.21 110M), we stroll below cliffs that have dropped some distressingly large blocks of rock into woods on our right. 175 metres after passing a small cave, at the next sharp left-hand bend, we leave the track for the final time (Wp.22 117M), then fork left twice in the next 150 metres (Wps.23 & 24).

distressingly large blocks of rock

After a serpentine descent through a stretch of woodland so deep and

the last Lime Kiln

dense and steep it's almost like we're spiralling into some pit at the bottom of the world, the gradient eases as we pass our last limekiln, which isn't particularly spectacular but might be sentimentally significant. 75 metres later, we fork right at a Y-junction (Wp.25 135M), then turn right 50 metres after that (Wp.26) to follow a new fence down to cross the end of the lane that climbs the **Son Marc** valley (Wp.27 139M). The path rejoins the lane 300 metres later (Wp.28 144M), at which point we simply bear left and follow the lane all the way to the MA-10.

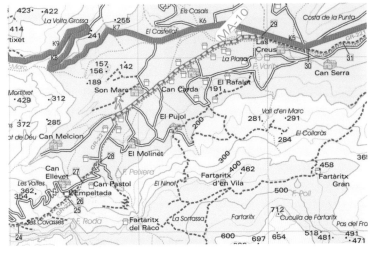

karst in Son Marc valley

karst on Serra d'en Massot

When the lane joins the MA-10 (Wp.29 176M), we bear right and follow

Son Marc

a scruffy path running parallel to the road alongside the **Torrent de la Vall d'en Marc**. Road and walking trail diverge 400 metres later, 50 metres after which we ignore a track crossing a bridge on our right for the 'Vall de Pollença Agroturisme' (Wp.30) and continue along the left bank of the torrent. 350 metres later, a short stretch of the path has been washed away, so we clamber onto the wall on our left where it broadens to a raised stone-clad 'road' (Wp.31 191M). Descending almost immediately via a rough wooden ladder off to our right, we cross a dirt track beside a bridge, after which we continue our pleasant riverside stroll.

Torrent de la Vall d'en Marc

By-passing a fence (a remnant of the days when this route was contested), we traverse a patch of eroded river bank via some wonderfully haphazard wooden steps, shortly after which we cross a dirt track beside a ford. 350 metres later, we reach a ford across an affluent (Wp.32 202M) and turn left to join the MA-10, which we follow to the right (on a path but cheek-by-jowl with the road) for 600 metres - just long enough to give an idea how unpleasant this stretch used to be.

haphazard wooden steps

At the km2.8 metre-stone (Wp.33 212M), we take a dirt track that shadows the road before joining a lane a little under 100 metres later. The lane swings right after 175 metres, at which point we carry straight on along a dirt track (Wp.34 215M). When the track dips down into a ford, we cross a new footbridge and turn left on a broad lane (Wp.35), which we follow for a kilometre until it arrives in **Pollença** beside the **Pont Romá** refuge (Wp.36 225M).

That's it. Done it!

'Done It!'

Playa Formentor

Pont Roma

It's always hard to end an LDP and, often as not, the first instinct is simply to do it all over again. I know a couple who walked the length of the Pyrenees along the GR11 on the Spanish side of the range, took one look at the Atlantic, then briskly did an about turn and headed east again. Didn't even cross the border to follow the GR10 on the French side. Just did the same trail again, all 600 kilometres of it. And when the Mediterranean hove into view, they still hadn't had enough, so they hung a right, picked up the GR7 and headed south to their home in Alicante. If the guy hadn't got himself gored by a disgruntled *toro bravo* in the back country of Valencia, I half suspect they'd still be walking now.

However, such Titan exploits (I'm talking about the walking, not being gored by a bull) are a luxury few of us can afford in our time-pressed era and most of you will probably have to call it quits when you reach **Pollença**, which is no bad place to end our adventure, even if the **Pont Roma** refuge is, somewhat distressingly, located in a converted abattoir - I shall resist the obvious jokes; it's a very nice place.

Apart from the bridge the refuge is named after, the town itself boasts few ancient monuments, but it has an incredibly rich history, in which Egyptians, Phoenicians, Romans, Carthaginians, Arabs -basically anybody who ever got in a boat in the Mediterranean- all played a part. It also appears to be the festival capital of **Mallorca** and, judging by the listings, you'd be unlucky to turn up when there wasn't some cultural event taking place. When you're checking what's on, don't be surprised if you click on a site aimed at a British audience and see an image of Agatha Christie pop up. She used to be a regular visitor, even wrote a short story called *Problem at Pollensa Bay*, and has recently been selected as 'the face of Pollença' by the local authorities.

If you have time and wish to move your body rather than your mind, there are plenty of things to be done at this end of the island, notably some fabulous walks and bathing opportunities along **Cap Formentor** (see 'Walk! Mallorca North & Mountains' Walks 36-40), a grand little climb

Cala san Vicenç

up the grand little hill of **Puig de Maria** immediately south of the town (see 'Walk! Mallorca North & Mountains' Walk 33), and there's even a British run diving school for those who feel like a change of element.

If you're not staying at the refuge, local specialists recommend the hotels Son Santjordi, Posada de Lluc, and Monnaber Nou and, wherever you're staying, we recommend the Tienda Bon Cami in **Port de Pollença**, where you can replace your dry-stone battered boots with something from the superb range of Mallorcan-made Bestard footwear, or indeed get just about anything else anyone who ever ventured into the mountains could want.

Puig Maria

To reach the bus station from the refuge, take 'Carrer de l'Horta' into town and carry straight on at every junction for the next 500 metres. When you reach a small square behind the church, bear left then right to take 'Carrer de Coronel Aloy' out of the 'Placeta Martorell'. Thereafter, follow the traffic signs for the town centre until you reach a large, cypress lined square ('Carrer del Convent') in front of the local museum. Cross the square to the diagonally opposite corner and take 'Carrer de Sant Domingo' to the left of 'Esglesia de la Mer de Deu de Roser'. The bus stop is on the right 150 metres later, directly below **Puig de Maria**. It's on the far side of town from the refuge, so allow at least 15 minutes to get there. Depending upon the frequency of stops en route, the bus trip to **Palma** takes between 30 and 45 minutes.

For more information, see:
www.thepollensaguide.com a very thorough English language guide featuring events, weather, photos, maps, shops, services, festivals etc
www.puerto-pollenca.costasur.com
. . . decidedly more .com than .net or .org, but a useful general site

This glossary contains Spanish and Catalán words found in the text (shown in *italics*) plus other local words that you may encounter. Please note that the spelling of place names and other local words on signs and maps can vary according to local conventions.

SPANISH	CATALÁN	
a		
agua, con/sin gas		water, fizzy/still
aljibe	**aljub**	ancient cistern/reservoir
alto	**dalt**	high, upper
área recreativa		picnic spot, usually with barbecues, toilets, water
atalaya		ancient watch-tower
avenida	**avinguda**	avenue
ayuntamiento	**ayuntament**	town hall
b		
bajo	**baix**	low
bajo	**avall**	lower
barranco	**barranc**	gorge, ravine
botadores		stone steps in country walls
c		
cala		creek, small bay, sometimes just a tiny coastal indentation
cala		inlet, cove
calle	**carrer**	street
camino	**camí**	road, path or way
camino real	**camí real**	royal road, once a major donkey trail
campo		countryside, field
canaleta	**siquia**	man-made water channel, including anything from a concrete canal to delicately arched aqueducts
carritx		pampas-like grass
casa	**can/ca**	house of (as *chez* in French)
casa de nieve	**casa neu**	snow pit/ice house
caseta		hut, cabin, small house
cingles		cliffs, crags; most often used to describe the sort of short, abrupt cliffs that typically define the rounded summits of many Catalán and Mallorcan mountains
ciudad	**ciutat**	city
coll		saddle, neck or pass
correos		post office
costa		coast
e		
embalse		reservoir
ermita		hermitage, small church, shrine
f		
faro		lighthouse
fiesta		festival, public holiday
finca	**lluc**	farm
forn de calc	**horno de calç**	lime kiln
fuente	**font**	spring, well
l		
lavadero		public laundry area
llano	**pla**	plain, flat land
m		
medio	**mig**	middle
mercado	**mercat**	market

mirador		viewing point, sometimes with man-made facilities, more often a natural place with a good view
morro		snout or muzzle, a rounded summit

p

parada		bus stop
particular		private
paseo	**passeig**	walkway
paso		pass
peatones		pedestrians
peña	**penya/penyal**	rock or boulder, used for a knoll or pinnacle on a ridge
pico	**puig**	translates as 'hill' or 'height', though more often a peak or mountain
pista		dirt road
pista forestal		forest road
playa	**platja**	beach
plaza	**plaça**	town square
pozo	**pou**	well
privado		private
prohibido el paso		no entry
puerto	**port**	port, mountain pass

r

refugio		mountain refuge, some offering basic overnight accommodation
rota		smallholding

s

santo/a	**san/sant**	saint
santuario	**santuari**	monastery, hermitage
sendero	**senda**	footpath, trail
sitja (pl. sitjes)	**sitja**	charcoal burning area or circle
su	**son, sa, ses**	his, her, their

t

tipico		typical, locals' café/bar
toro bravo		wild bull
torre		tower, often a coastal watchtower built to warn of approaching pirates, or a Moorish lookout tower
torrente	**torrent**	stream

u

urbanización		housing development

Distances are given in kilometres, ascents (A) and descents (D) in metres. The ascents and descents are calculated from our own GPS records. GPS does not measure altitude as accurately as it does latitude and longitude, but rather than estimating climbs and ascents, I've stuck with our measurements, even when this implies a slight discrepancy or illogicality between comparable alternatives.

Vital Statistics GR221 Port d'Andratx to Pollença (official route)
Total distance 115km, total ascents (A) 4750 metres, total descents (D) 5015 metres.

Stage One
a. Port d'Andratx to St. Elm (all services) 7km   A300   D300
b. St. Elm
        to Sa Trapa (future refuge)   3.03km A285 D25
        to S'Arraco turn off (no services) 6.35km A420 D120
        to S'Arraco (all services)   11.3km A500 D420
Alternative Stage 1A
Es Capdella to Stage 2 Wp.30 (1h from Estellencs) 8.75km A480 D450
Alternative Stage 1B
Puigpunyent to Estellencs (all services) 8km A400 D500
Stage Two
S'Arraco turn off to Pla s'Evangelica (no services, link for campers) 4.7km A40 D80
Pla s'Evangelica to Coma d'en Vidal refuge (closed, but water & shelter) 6.5km A550 D270
        to Estellencs (all services) 12km A550 D700
Stage Three
A. Estellencs to Banyalbufar (all services) 3km on foot + 3km hitching A120 D165
B. Banyalbufar to Esporles (all services) 6.9km A330 D260
Stage Four
A. Esporles to Valldemossa (all services) 8.2km A570 D360
B. Valldemossa to Deià (all services, including first refuge)   7.9km A520 D800
Stage Five Deià
        to Son Micó & Son Bleda (hotels) 5km A 250 D 100
        to La Muleta   (refuge) 8.5km A 250 D 250
        to Port de Sóller (all services) 10km A 250   D 350 (excluding Muleta spur)
        to Sóller (all services) 12.5km 280 D 415 (excluding Muleta spur)
Stage Six
A. Sóller to Cúber / Font des Noguer (picnic area, water point, barbecues,

camping possible, seasonal bus-stop) 10.5km   A 880   D 140 NB The Cuber refuge at the western end of the reservoir is unmanned and locked. However, if you're surprised by bad weather, you may want to stop at the refuge, since it does have a covered porch for shelter.

B. Cúber to Font des Prat turn-off (start of Stage 7 description) 2.5km A 50 D 30

to Tossals Verds via Coll d'es Coloms (official route of the GR) (refuge) 5.3km A80 D230

to Tossals Verds via Coll de sa Coma des Ases & Pas Llis (refuge) 4.75km A150 D410

Stage Seven

A. Tossals Verds to Font des Prat turn-off (start of Stage 7 description) 3km A200 D negligible

B. Font des Prat turn-off to Lluc (refuge, monastery, campsite, restaurants, chemist, ATM machine, information centre, bus stop) 11km A330 D780

Stage Eight

Lluc to Pollença (all services) 14.5km   A160 D635

The following list is not exhaustive. Our experience of staying in Mallorcan hotels is minimal, but as a rule, even the cheapest rooms are generally clean and adequate. Apart from Stage Five, when I would imagine most people will want to continue into Sóller, I recommend staying in the refuges after Deià (Stage Four), though you may wish to treat yourself to one of the more upmarket recommended options in Pollença.

* Reader recommended ** Recommended by local tourism specialists

Refuge Prices:

Accommodation per person 11€,
Double Room (only at Tossals Verds)   39€
'Extras':- Sheets 3€, Towels 1€, Breakfast 4.50€, Lunch 10.50€, Dinner 8€, Salad 4.50€, Children's menu 5€, Picnic 6.50€.

To book refuges on-line, visit the relevant page of the Consell de Mallorca's site:

www.conselldemallorca.cat/mediambient/pedra/senderisme.php?o pcio=20&reserva=1

Accommodation in La Palma:

www.laminosa.com www.terminushostal.com In the bus station and recommended by Lonely Planet, www.hostalbrondo.com www.hostalreginapalma.com Near the Plaza d'Espanya bus station; www.hotelmisiondesanmiguel.com Near the Plaza d'Espanya bus station.

Accommodation on Stage One

Port d'Andratx; www.hatjam.com/catalinavera
www.hotelmonport.com www.hotelvillaitalia.com.

Sant Elm ;www.hostaldragonera.net

S'Arraco; Casa Maria on www.mallorcabandb.com
www.hotelescaleta.com
Andratx; www.sonesteve.com
Accommodation on Stage Two
Coma d'en Vidal Refuge (ready for use, but yet to be opened at the time of
going to press)
Estellencs; www.terra.es/personal4/phsaplana
www.hotelruralnord.com www.mallorcaonline.com/hotel/maristu
www.pangea.org/olivar
Accommodation on Stage Three
Banyalbufar; www.hostalcanbusquets.com www.hotelmarivent.com
www.hbaronia.com A magnificent old house with superb sea views that
would ordinarily be the preserve of a clutch of stars and stratospheric
prices. www.hotelsacoma.com www.sonborguny.com
www.camadopaula.com
Esporles; www.agroturismo-alfatx.com www.hotelestada.com
Pricey, but good value. This is the only hotel actually in Esporles. The
others are *agroturismos* in the countryside.
www.parcdecanet.com www.cantorna.com www.posada-marques.com
Accommodation on Stage Four
Valldemossa; www.hostalcanmario.net
www.hostalcanmario.iespana.es www.espetithotel-valldemossa.com
www.mirabo.es www.valldemossahotel.com
Deià; Can Boi Refuge,
www.pensionmiramar.com www.hostalvillaverde.com
www.hoteldespuig.com www.esmoli.com **
www.hotel-laresidencia.com **
Accommodation on Stage Five
La Muleta Refuge
son.mico@hotmail.com A wing of Can Prohom, the famous farmhouse
above Sóller on the route of the GR221.
www.sonbleda.de Luxury hotel opposite Can Prohom
Port de Sóller; www.hotelportosoller.com *
www.hotelesport.com ** www.hotelmarinasoller.com *
www.hoteleden.com www.hotel-brisas.com **
www.hotel-losgeranios.com
Muleta de ca s'Hereu see 'Fincas' on www.agroturismo-balear.com O n
the GR midway between the Muleta turn-off and Port de Sóller
www.esplendidohotel.com www.canai.com On the GR between Port de
Sóller and Sóller
Sóller; Hostal Nadal at hostalresinadal@wanadoo.es
Casa de Huespedes Margarita Trias no website. Tel. (00 34) 971 634 214
www.casa-bougainvillea.com hotelelguia@gmail.com
www.sollernet.com/sardeviu www.lavilahotel.com
www.hotelcalbisbe.com www.canisabel.com
www.cascurial.com On our 'round the houses' route
www.avenida-hotel.com www.granhotelsoller.com
www.hotelsalvia.com

Accommodation on Stage Six Tossals Verds Refuge

Accommodation on Stage Seven Son Amer Refuge
In the monastery www.lluc.net * **
Accommodation on Stage Eight Pont Roma Refuge
www.sonsantjordi.com www.hotelsantjordi.com **
www.posadadelluc.com ** www.monnaber.com **
Port de Pollença; www.hoposa.es/pagingles/hostalbahiai.htm *

Appendix C. Transport en route

Rather than reproducing pages and pages of timetables that might go out of date and have stranded walkers sending us angry letters of rebuke (always presuming said walkers got unstranded), I have simply selected the transport links that are most likely to be of use, but make no claim to their sempiternity. The service frequency reproduced here should be taken as a rough guide. It is essential to check the precise times of the services you intend using before making the definitive plan for your trip. You should bear in mind that weekend services are less frequent.

In theory, all Mallorcan bus services are now being coordinated by the TIB public transport network. In practice, private companies (like Villalonga which is based in the Northeast) still publish their own timetables and run buses in their own livery. The following information is intended as a selective guide to the services most useful for walkers and giving a rough idea of the services' regularity at their seasonal best (between May and October).

For detailed planning, see http://tib.caib.es for the TIB services (the L100s for the southwest, L200s for the central area, and L300s for the northeast) and www.autocaresmallorca.com for the Villalonga services (Linea 3 etc). Another useful site covering the northeast is www.puertopollensa.biz/bus_services_from_puerto_pollensa.htm. Double check on arrival by asking for up-to-date timetables from the Tourist Offices.

L100 Andratx - Port d'Andratx - s'Arracó - Sant Elm - every hour or two
L102 Palma - Andratx - Port d'Andratx - every half hour
L111 Palma - Calvià - es Capdella - every 2-3 hours - Sundays every 4 hours
L140 Palma - Puigpunyent - Galilea - every 2 hours - Weekends 3 per day; NB Passengers for Galilea must book by telephoning 971 430 515 the day before.
L200 Palma - Esporles - Banyalbufar - Estellencs - hourly
L210 Palma - Valldemossa - Deià - Sóller - every 2 hours
L211 Palma - Bunyola - Sóller - 15 buses per day
L320 Alaró - Palma (changing at Estació Consell) - hourly
L330 Palma - Selva - Caimari - Lluc - every 2 hours
L332 Inca - Selva - Caimari - Lluc - every 3 hours
L340 Palma - Inca - Pollença - twice an hour
Linea 3 Puerto Pollença - Formentor - 4 times a day
Linea 4 Pollença - Lluc - Sóller - twice a day

Linea 5 Pollença - Llluc - Calobra - once a day
NB Linea 5 leaves Pollença at 10.20, arrives in Lluc at 10.50, stops for an hour then reaches Calobra at12.45. Departs for the return at 3pm, leaving Lluc at 4pm. A local website suggests passengers picking up the return bus from Lluc should be at the stop well in advance as the bus "doesn't hang about on the way back"!

For additional information on transport see:
www.mallorca.com/english www.trasmediterranea.es
www.barcoszules.com   www.trendesoller.com

Appendix D. Links to other walks

See Walk! Mallorca North & Mountains (N&M) and Walk! Mallorca West (W) for these additional itineraries feeding into or adjacent to the GR221:-
Stage 1 (W) Walks 11-20, **Stage 2** (W) Walks 21-23,
Stage 3 (W) Walks 25, 27, & 28, **Stage 4** (N&M) Walks 2-7,
Stage 5 (N&M) Walks 1, 8, & 9, **Stage 6** (N&M) Walks 10-18,
Stage 7 (N&M) Walks 19, & 20-22, **Stage 8** (N&M) Walks 29-35

Appendix E. Miscellaneous information

Emergencies Tel. 112
For up-dates, see the updates section on Discovery Walking Guides' website at **www.walking.demon.co.uk** the news and GR221 pages on the very useful walking website run by a couple of Mallorcan mountain guides - **http://idd02ucg.eresmas.net/hike.htm** and the section of the local government site dealing with the GR221 **www.conselldemallorca.net/mediambient/pedra**.

For additional information, see www.mallorca.com/english
www.balearnet.com www.mallorcaservice.com www.caib.es
www.conselldemallorca.net www.apitmallorca.com

Highly recommended is the excellent Bon Cami Trekking, Outdoor and Adventure shop stocking a wide range of books, clothing and equipment (Calle Roger de Flor 36, Port de Pollença www.boncami.com).

Calzados Bestard (c/Estación 40-42, Lloseta www.bestard.com) make excellent walking boots. Apart from their children's line, all their boots, shoes and sandals are made locally, and they even have a resoling service if your favourite Bestard boots are just too comfy to give up when the Vibram grip begins to wear out. If you can't get to their factory shop, their products are available at Bon Cami (see above).

Using GPS on Mallorca's GR221

The GPS Waypoint lists are as recorded by Charles during his research of the GR221. In the interests of clarity, each map section only shows the waypoints for that Stage. For readers wondering what we are talking about, GPS Waypoints are also Grid References to the exact locations within each walking route, when used in conjunction with the **Mallorca (North & Mountains) Tour & Trail Map 5th edition**.

GPS Waypoints are subject to the general considerations as to the accuracy of GPS units in the location concerned. Mallorca's GR221 generally has good GPS reception though one exception is along the *Barranc de Biniaraitx* where there is only one logical way so your navigational accuracy will not be compromised.

To Input the Waypoints

Waypoint co-ordinates are quoted for the WGS84 datum, used to provide grid references on the Tour & Trail Map, in degrees and minutes of Latitude and Longitude. To input the waypoints into your GPS we suggest that you:

- switch on your GPS and select 'simulator' (or 'gps off') mode
- check that your GPS is set to the WGS84 datum (its default datum) and the 'location format' 'hddd°.mm..mmmm'
- input the GPS waypoints into a 'route' file with the same number as the Stage number; then when you call up the 'Stage' on the GR221 there will be no confusion as to which walking route it refers to.
- repeat the inputting of waypoints into 'routes' until you have covered all the stages you plan to walk.
- turn off your GPS. When you turn the GPS back on it should return to its normal navigation mode.

Waypoints are provided as an additional navigation aid to complement the detailed walk descriptions. Knowing exactly where you are in relation to our detailed walk description is a great confidence booster when exploring these new and exciting landscapes. GPS Waypoints are provided for all key navigational points on all Stages of the GR221; never again should you find yourself wondering whether you are on the right path or not.

Personal Navigator Files (PNFs).

Edited versions of all the GPS tracks and waypoints compiled during Charles Davis' research are available on our **Personal Navigator Files CD version 5.01.** GPS Utility Special edition software is included on the CD, enabling the user to load track and waypoint information direct to their GPS unit via a PC. In addition to the **GR221 Mallorca** our PNFs CD (5.01) contains the GPS tracks and waypoints for **Mallorca North & Mountains, Mallorca West, Menorca, La Gomera, La Palma, Tenerife, Lanzarote, Sierra de Aracena, Madeira, Alpujarras, Axarquia, Andorra, Brittany (North), Walks around Calais & Boulogne,** and the full **Walk! UK** series of guide books covering **Lake District North, Lake District South, Yorkshire Dales (North & Central), South Pennines, Peak District South, Brecon Beacons, South Downs, Dorset, Isle of Wight, Devon, Dartmoor** and **Exmoor.**

Waypoints are quoted for the WGS84 Datum, Lat/Long position format.

Stage 1A
Port d'Andratx - Sant Elm

Wpt	North	East
01	39 32.8902	02 23.0556
02	39 32.9826	02 23.0196
03	39 33.0096	02 22.8750
04	39 33.1566	02 22.7244
05	39 33.1722	02 22.7040
06	39 33.2268	02 22.6602
07	39 33.2832	02 22.3866
08	39 33.3138	02 22.3170
09	39 33.8310	02 22.5306
10	39 34.0314	02 22.4706
11	39 34.1976	02 22.1292
12	39 34.2012	02 22.0764
13	39 34.3182	02 22.1250
14	39 34.3008	02 22.0668
15	39 34.3032	02 22.0212
16	39 34.2570	02 21.8844
17	39 34.2144	02 21.6102
18	39 34.3884	02 21.3648
19	39 34.3608	02 21.3006
20	39 34.3908	02 21.2172
21	39 34.4688	02 21.2352

Stage 1B
Sant Elm - La Trapa & S'Arraco

Wpt	North	East
01	39 34.6818	02 21.2592
02	39 34.7520	02 21.0294
03	39 34.7802	02 21.0186
04	39 34.9956	02 20.9820
05	39 35.0304	02 21.0252
06	39 35.0904	02 21.1680
07	39 35.1324	02 21.2352
08	39 35.3160	02 21.3000
09	39 35.4018	02 21.3102
10	39 35.5104	02 21.3408
11	39 35.5542	02 21.4416
12	39 35.6064	02 21.5028
13	39 35.8290	02 21.5412
14	39 35.8650	02 21.5400
15	39 35.9580	02 21.6576
16	39 36.0234	02 21.8436
17	39 36.4104	02 22.2744
18	39 36.5952	02 22.2102
19	39 36.6132	02 22.1358
20	39 36.6006	02 22.6884
21	39 36.5310	02 22.8354
22	39 36.5094	02 22.8852
23	39 36.4896	02 22.9188
24	39 36.4500	02 23.0046
25	39 36.2730	02 22.8690
26	39 36.2502	02 22.9902
27	39 36.1044	02 23.0412
28	39 35.9442	02 23.0676
29	39 35.7828	02 23.0310
30	39 35.4438	02 22.7754
31	39 35.3832	02 23.1294
32	39 35.2830	02 23.1036
33	39 34.7694	02 23.5974

Alt Stage 1A
Es Capdella - Estellencs

Wpt	North	East
01	39 34.7766	02 28.1466
02	39 35.0352	02 28.2006
03	39 35.9154	02 28.3542
04	39 36.1566	02 28.2708
05	39 36.4092	02 28.2252
06	39 36.7050	02 28.0218
07	39 37.4268	02 27.9222
08	39 37.5426	02 27.8562
09	39 37.6392	02 27.8418
10	39 37.7838	02 27.7368
11	39 37.9620	02 27.6390
12	39 38.0148	02 27.6048
13	39 38.0406	02 27.7068
14	39 38.2302	02 27.8406
15	39 38.2848	02 27.9204
16	39 38.3988	02 28.0440
17	39 38.4954	02 28.1208
18	39 38.6142	02 28.0710
0230	39 38.6994	02 27.9192
0231	39 38.7744	02 27.8202
0232	39 38.8380	02 27.9396
0233	39 38.9052	02 27.8190
0234	39 38.9502	02 28.0770
0235	39 39.1092	02 28.1472
0236	39 39.0240	02 28.2930
0237	39 39.1488	02 28.3434
0238	39 39.1074	02 28.5822
0239	39 39.1560	02 28.8420

Alt Stage 1B
Puigpunyent - Estellencs

Wpt	North	East
01	39 37.8078	02 31.5756
02	39 38.1444	02 31.0482
03	39 38.1222	02 30.9762
04	39 38.1240	02 30.7248
05	39 38.3472	02 30.6438
06	39 38.4618	02 30.5736
07	39 38.5884	02 30.4980
08	39 38.6778	02 30.5694
09	39 38.7744	02 30.6012
10	39 38.8176	02 30.5994
11	39 38.8854	02 30.6264
12	39 38.8554	02 30.4272
13	39 38.8164	02 30.2994

14	39 38.7948	02 30.2028
15	39 38.9286	02 30.2520
16	39 38.9310	02 30.2184
17	39 38.9868	02 30.0504
18	39 38.9628	02 29.9514
19	39 38.9862	02 29.9766
20	39 38.8806	02 29.5866
21	39 38.9082	02 29.3850
22	39 38.9946	02 29.3790
23	39 39.0822	02 29.2164
24	39 39.0912	02 29.1480
25	39 39.2034	02 29.0088

Stage 2
Ses Basses - Evangèlica link

Wpt	North	East
01	39 36.4506	02 23.0022
02	39 36.4800	02 23.2590
03	39 36.3558	02 23.5524
04	39 36.2808	02 24.5430
05	39 36.7068	02 24.9210
06	39 36.9510	02 25.1892

Stage 2
Evangèlica - Estellencs

Wpt	North	East
01	39 36.9480	02 25.1868
02	39 36.9576	02 25.4148
03	39 36.9858	02 25.4436
04	39 37.0692	02 25.5318
05	39 37.1010	02 25.5924
06	39 37.1604	02 25.6962
07	39 37.1934	02 25.6896
08	39 37.2108	02 25.6038
09	39 37.2942	02 25.7172
10	39 37.3494	02 25.8270
11	39 37.3332	02 25.9998
12	39 37.3482	02 26.1510
13	39 37.3356	02 26.2686
14	39 37.4784	02 26.2230
15	39 37.5900	02 26.2062
16	39 37.6206	02 26.2368
17	39 37.6272	02 26.3058
18	39 37.6902	02 26.3094
19	39 37.6230	02 26.4186
20	39 37.6014	02 26.6658
21	39 37.7628	02 26.7102
22	39 37.8030	02 26.7996
23	39 37.7940	02 26.8806
24	39 37.8000	02 26.9268
25	39 37.7700	02 27.0192
26	39 37.7868	02 27.2034
27	39 37.9368	02 27.3948
28	39 38.1708	02 27.2802
29	39 38.3352	02 27.3516
30	39 38.6994	02 27.9192
31	39 38.7744	02 27.8202
32	39 38.8380	02 27.9396
33	39 38.9052	02 27.8190
34	39 38.9502	02 28.0770

35	39 39.1092	02 28.1472
36	39 39.0240	02 28.2930
37	39 39.1488	02 28.3434
38	39 39.1074	02 28.5822
39	39 39.1560	02 28.8420

Stage 3A
Estellencs - Banyalbufar

Wpt	North	East
01	39 39.2076	02 29.0166
02	39 39.3114	02 29.0418
03	39 39.3354	02 29.1006
04	39 39.5322	02 29.0544
05	39 39.7764	02 29.2698
06	39 39.8418	02 29.2236
07	39 39.8310	02 29.3166
08	39 39.9036	02 29.3346
09	39 40.2144	02 29.6022
10	39 40.3774	02 29.6958
11	39 41.1630	02 30.7470

Stage 3B
Banyalbufar - Esporles

Wpt	North	East
01	39 41.2314	02 30.8220
02	39 40.9230	02 31.7832
03	39 40.8330	02 31.7790
04	39 40.7814	02 32.5656
05	39 40.8084	02 32.7072
06	39 40.6638	02 32.8560
07	39 40.6056	02 33.1230
08	39 40.4226	02 33.2730
09	39 40.3590	02 33.6366
10	39 40.1304	02 34.0674
11	39 40.1190	02 34.2690
12	39 40.1304	02 34.5114
13	39 40.1136	02 34.6530

Stage 4A
Esporles - Vall demossa

Wpt	North	East
01	39 40.1304	02 34.6482
02	39 40.1958	02 34.7454
03	39 40.2420	02 34.8762
04	39 40.3770	02 35.1540
05	39 40.4910	02 35.2026
06	39 40.8444	02 34.9596
07	39 41.1690	02 35.7258
08	39 41.0790	02 35.8086
09	39 41.1504	02 35.8776
10	39 41.1834	02 35.8734
11	39 41.2872	02 35.9136
12	39 41.2710	02 36.0684
13	39 41.2866	02 36.1158
14	39 41.3460	02 36.0768
15	39 41.5020	02 35.9724
16	39 41.5326	02 35.9292
17	39 41.6088	02 35.9598
18	39 41.6094	02 36.1308

19	39 41.8320	02 36.2916
20	39 41.9646	02 36.2202
21	39 42.0228	02 36.1698
22	39 42.0738	02 36.2796
23	39 42.0894	02 36.4692
24	39 42.1284	02 36.5400
25	39 42.2166	02 36.6570
26	39 42.2634	02 36.8142
27	39 42.4680	02 37.0440
28	39 42.4860	02 37.0668
29	39 42.5376	02 37.2036
30	39 42.5964	02 37.2468

Stage 4B
Valledemossa - Deià

Wpt	North	East
01	39 42.6036	02 37.2342
02	39 42.6498	02 37.1430
03	39 42.7206	02 37.1778
04	39 42.8406	02 37.2894
05	39 42.9696	02 37.3722
06	39 43.3608	02 37.2336
07	39 43.6908	02 37.3368
08	39 43.6068	02 37.4586
09	39 43.8570	02 37.9476
10	39 44.0478	02 38.0310
11	39 44.1594	02 38.1360
12	39 44.1564	02 38.0304
13	39 44.2530	02 38.0820
14	39 44.3232	02 38.0598
15	39 44.3328	02 38.1588
16	39 44.3532	02 38.1294
17	39 44.5440	02 38.0766
18	39 44.4474	02 38.0862
19	39 44.4222	02 38.1174
20	39 44.7048	02 38.4288
21	39 44.8260	02 38.6058
22	39 44.8464	02 38.5614
23	39 44.8362	02 38.5308
24	39 44.7876	02 38.7372

Stage 5
Deià - Sóller

Wpt	North	East
01	39 44.7822	02 38.7414
02	39 44.7984	02 38.8692
03	39 44.9406	02 38.9058
04	39 45.0540	02 38.7966
05	39 45.2304	02 38.5788
06	39 45.4092	02 38.5512
07	39 45.4578	02 38.6868
08	39 45.4764	02 38.8698
09	39 45.5772	02 39.0258
10	39 45.6198	02 39.1266
11	39 45.8682	02 39.6630
12	39 45.8934	02 39.7878
13	39 45.9036	02 39.8136
14	39 46.2894	02 40.4670
15	39 46.2984	02 40.6428
16	39 46.4178	02 40.5912

17	39 46.4742	02 40.5792
18	39 46.7886	02 40.4652
19	39 46.8714	02 40.4928
20	39 46.9038	02 40.6200
21	39 47.1120	02 40.7790
22	39 47.3184	02 40.7742
23	39 47.5206	02 40.8078
24	39 47.7432	02 40.8438
25	39 47.7924	02 40.8756
26	39 47.0994	02 40.8330
27	39 47.0964	02 40.8558
28	39 47.0316	02 40.8738
29	39 47.0874	02 41.1648
30	39 47.0754	02 41.3562
31	39 47.0754	02 41.5092
32	39 47.1078	02 41.7540
33	39 47.0412	02 41.8494
34	39 46.7820	02 41.7342
35	39 46.7022	02 41.6244
36	39 46.3740	02 42.2052
37	39 46.4160	02 42.3324
38	39 46.3782	02 42.4836
39	39 46.3086	02 42.5940
40	39 46.4394	02 42.6756
41	39 46.4028	02 42.6948
42	39 46.3932	02 42.9060
43	39 46.3026	02 42.0164
44	39 46.3272	02 42.1794
45	39 46.2528	02 42.3654
46	39 46.1754	02 42.4152
47	39 46.0338	02 42.5382
48	39 46.1040	02 42.7158
49	39 45.9762	02 42.8352
50	39 45.9990	02 42.9342
51	39 46.0296	02 42.9726
52	39 46.1232	02 42.9354

Stage 6A
Sóller - Cúber

Wpt	North	East
01	39 46.3002	02 43.0218
02	39 46.3506	02 43.1784
03	39 46.4064	02 43.1730
04	39 46.4436	02 43.3128
05	39 46.6170	02 43.5624
06	39 46.6356	02 43.5480
07	39 46.6272	02 43.7094
08	39 46.4262	02 43.8132
09	39 46.4214	02 43.8462
10	39 46.3308	02 44.0184
11	39 46.2720	02 44.0886
12	39 46.2852	02 44.1678
13	39 46.1832	02 44.2542
14	39 46.0416	02 44.3520
15	39 46.0428	02 44.4804
16	39 45.9924	02 44.9346
17	39 45.8988	02 45.1884
18	39 45.7422	02 45.3690
19	39 45.5646	02 45.3546
20	39 45.5970	02 45.4008

21	39 45.6546	02 45.5712
22	39 45.6438	02 45.5886
23	39 45.7626	02 45.6480
24	39 45.9024	02 45.7182
25	39 45.8970	02 45.7386
26	39 45.9624	02 45.7812
27	39 46.1874	02 46.0824
28	39 46.6860	02 46.7052
29	39 47.2344	02 47.8098

Stage 6B
Cúber - Tossals Verds (official)

Wpt	North	East
01	39 47.2344	02 47.8122
02	39 47.2206	02 47.9484
03	39 47.2452	02 47.9754
04	39 47.5266	02 49.4292
05	39 47.3100	02 49.5246
06	39 47.2542	02 49.7034
07	39 47.1048	02 49.8786
08	39 46.6146	02 49.8264
09	39 46.4568	02 49.7598
10	39 46.2246	02 49.4916
11	39 46.1370	02 49.3434
12	39 46.1940	02 49.1688
13	39 46.1292	02 49.1688

Stage 6B Alt
Cúber - Tossals Verds (via Pas Llis)

Wpt	North	East
01	39 47.2344	02 47.8122
02	39 47.2098	02 47.8680
03	39 47.0706	02 48.0636
04	39 47.0304	02 48.1806
05	39 46.8900	02 48.1860
06	39 46.6608	02 48.1128
07	39 46.6182	02 48.1854
08	39 46.5714	02 48.1944
09	39 46.4898	02 48.2730
10	39 46.4388	02 48.5268
11	39 46.2714	02 48.8232
12	39 46.3206	02 49.0920
13	39 46.1850	02 49.1052

Stage 7B
Font des Prats - Lluc

Wpt	North	East
01	39 47.2542	02 49.7064
02	39 47.3016	02 49.7538
03	39 47.3742	02 49.8456
04	39 47.7192	02 50.1900
05	39 47.9346	02 50.3388
06	39 47.9790	02 50.3526
07	39 48.1464	02 50.5704
08	39 48.3348	02 50.8296
09	39 48.3978	02 50.9940
10	39 48.5118	02 51.1224
11	39 48.6894	02 51.1560
12	39 48.6534	02 51.3786
13	39 48.8070	02 51.6624
14	39 48.8178	02 51.3966
15	39 48.9126	02 51.2646
16	39 48.9270	02 51.4848
17	39 49.0164	02 51.6330
18	39 49.1160	02 51.9234
19	39 49.1040	02 52.0302
20	39 49.0854	02 52.2642
21	39 49.0926	02 52.3128
22	39 49.2372	02 52.3368
23	39 49.2090	02 52.8060
24	39 49.1730	02 53.0094
25	39 49.3080	02 53.2182
26	39 49.1154	02 53.4972

Stage 8
Lluc - Pollença

Wpt	North	East
01	39 49.0146	02 53.6268
02	39 48.9846	02 53.7060
03	39 48.9696	02 53.9136
04	39 49.0608	02 54.1218
05	39 49.1040	02 54.2124
06	39 49.1850	02 54.2316
07	39 49.2276	02 54.2436
08	39 49.2744	02 54.2106
09	39 49.2846	02 54.2310
10	39 49.3242	02 54.2616
11	39 49.3980	02 54.2508
12	39 49.6080	02 54.5124
13	39 50.0286	02 54.7332
14	39 50.3310	02 54.5400
15	39 50.5242	02 54.5922
16	39 50.8698	02 54.8976
17	39 51.0168	02 55.1838
18	39 51.0048	02 55.3512
19	39 51.0894	02 55.5042
20	39 51.1008	02 55.5990
21	39 51.0714	02 55.6698
22	39 51.0822	02 55.9440
23	39 51.0762	02 55.9788
24	39 51.0642	02 56.0448
25	39 51.2028	02 56.4306
26	39 51.2292	02 56.4756
27	39 51.2784	02 56.5464
28	39 51.4176	02 56.6922
29	39 52.1304	02 58.0008
30	39 52.0452	02 58.3356
31	39 52.0788	02 58.5750
32	39 52.3236	02 59.1408
33	39 52.4928	02 59.5962
34	39 52.5162	02 59.7834
35	39 52.6884	03 00.1644
36	39 52.9464	03 00.8154